Frank J Bramhall

The Military Souvenir

A portrait gallery of our military and naval heroes

Frank J Bramhall

The Military Souvenir
A portrait gallery of our military and naval heroes

ISBN/EAN: 9783337213756

Printed in Europe, USA, Canada, Australia, Japan

Cover: Foto ©ninafisch / pixelio.de

More available books at **www.hansebooks.com**

THE Military Souvenir.

THE MILITARY SOUVENIR;

A Portrait Gallery of OUR MILITARY & NAVAL HEROES.

By Frank J. Bramhall.

Illustrated with Engravings on Steel.

Vol. I.

NEW YORK:
J. C. BUTTRE, 48 FRANKLIN STREET.
MDCCCLXIII.

THE
Military Souvenir;

A

PORTRAIT GALLERY

OF

OUR MILITARY AND NAVAL HEROES.

By Frank J. Bramhall.

> "Their armor rings on a nobler field
>   Than the Greek and the Trojan fiercely trod,
> For Freedom's sword is the blade they wield,
>   And the light above is the smile of God.
> So, in his isle of calm delight,
>   Jason may sleep the years away,
> For THE HEROES LIVE, and the sky is bright,
>   And the world is a braver world to-day."
>
> — EDNA DEAN PROCTOR.

Illustrated with 75 Engravings on Steel.

NEW YORK:
J. C. BUTTRE, 48 FRANKLIN STREET.
MDCCCLXIII.

TO

THE NOBLE

Defenders of our Country

THIS VOLUME

IS

RESPECTFULLY DEDICATED.

PREFACE.

> "It then remains,
> That you do speak to the people."

"WHAT is more agreeable to the curiosity of the mind and the eye," asks D'Israeli, "than the portraits of great characters? An old philosopher whom Marville invited to see a collection of landscapes by a celebrated artist, replied: 'Landscapes I prefer seeing in the country itself, but I am fond of contemplating the pictures of illustrious men.'" There is much truth in this opinion, and we hope the American people may not be exceeded in this respect by the old philosopher.

D'Israeli also says: "A taste for collecting portraits, or busts, was warmly pursued in the happier periods of Rome; for the celebrated Atticus, in a work he published of illustrious Romans, made it more delightful by ornamenting it with the portraits of those great men; and the learned Varro, in his biography of Seven Hundred Celebrated Men, by giving the world their true features and their physiognomy, in some manner—*aliquo modo imaginibus* is Pliny's expression—showed that even their persons should not entirely be annihilated. 'They, indeed,' adds Pliny, 'form a spectacle which the gods themselves might contemplate; for if the gods sent those heroes to the earth, it is Varro who secured their immortality, and has so multiplied and distributed them in all places, that we may carry them about us, place them wherever we choose, and fix our eyes on them with perpetual admiration—a spectacle that every day becomes more varied and interesting, as new heroes appear, and as works of this kind are spread abroad.'" So applicable are these words that they need no comment. Their peculiar bearing upon a work like this is at once patent to every eye.

None have greater claims upon a nation than they who fight and bleed in defence of her and her liberties. None have greater claims upon the world and humanity than they who do righteous battle in Freedom's holy cause. These men whose portraits we now give to the world have fought and bled in defence of the best government the sun ever shone upon, established upon the great and never-dying principle that "ALL MEN ARE CREATED EQUAL; THAT THEY ARE ENDOWED BY THEIR CREATOR WITH CERTAIN UNALIENABLE RIGHTS; THAT AMONG THESE ARE LIFE, LIBERTY, AND THE PURSUIT OF HAPPINESS." What, therefore, could be more outrageous than an attempt to forcibly rend asunder and destroy such a nation, and to found on its ruins an aristocratic oligarchy? They, then, who sprang to arms to put down this hideous

PREFACE.

rebellion, fight not only for a nation but for the world, for mankind, and for Freedom. Men never fought in a nobler cause, nor beneath a holier banner, than do these heroes of the Republic in this her great contest for Freedom and Nationality.

Not only are the features of those who still live to fight for our beloved country represented, but also those who have fallen in the good fight—who, though lost to us on earth, still plead our cause at the bar of God. They were too noble and too good for earth, and the Omnipotent has gathered them to their Father's bosom. There is young ELLSWORTH, the proto-martyr of our great cause; the sad, thoughtful face of WINTHROP, our Körner with sword and lyre; the chivalric LYON, our good knight "sans peur et sans reproche;" BAKER, our Senate's Cicero; "BOY BRITTAN," of whose brief but glorious career History's broad page scarcely affords a counterpart; the brave LANDER, to whom hardship and danger were but iotas in the path of duty; FOOT, the gift of Law to Freedom; WALLACE, whom Shiloh's bloody field will long remember; the youthful and the dashing HAINES; STEVENS, whose hand grasped our bright banner even in death; KEARNEY, the bravest of the brave; the gallant RENO, and the gray-haired MANSFIELD, whose bravery and valor South Mountain's gory heights do well attest; MITCHEL, now treading the stars he loved to gaze upon in life; God's earthly soldier, FULLER; FOOTE, the Christian warrior of our navy, who faced death calmly in his bed after braving many a roaring tempest and fiery battle-shock; the patient prisoner, CORCORAN; noble, pure-hearted, and beloved old WADSWORTH, as true a hero as ever fell bravely fighting in a righteous cause; and last, but not least, the gallant and impetuous MULLIGAN: "They pleased God, and He took them."

Of the excellence of the beautiful engravings which adorn and constitute perhaps the chief feature of this work, we need not speak. In correctness of portraiture they are unequalled, while as works of art, their delicate softness and fineness, and their elegance and superiority of finish, are plain to every eye.

In regard to the letter-press of the work, we would merely remark that it is written in a spirit of truthfulness and impartiality, and in the belief that good deeds are most deserving of record. Nothing is claimed in a literary point of view, as we aim only to give to the world and posterity the true records of these gallant defenders of our nationality, which we believe to be worthy of careful and attentive study.

F. J. B.

PLEASANT VALLEY, NEW YORK,
  December 25th, 1864.

Illustrations.

1. THE PRESIDENT & CABINET (Group)—FRONTISPIECE.
   ENGRAVED TITLE-PAGE (Extra).
2. GENERALS OF OUR ARMY (Group).
3. LIEUTENANT-GENERAL WINFIELD SCOTT.
4. LIEUTENANT-GENERAL ULYSSES S. GRANT.
5. MAJOR-GENERAL GEO. B. McCLELLAN.
6. MAJOR-GENERAL JOHN C. FREMONT.
7. MAJOR-GENERAL HENRY W. HALLECK.
8. MAJOR-GENERAL JOHN E. WOOL.
9. MAJOR-GENERAL JOHN A. DIX.
10. MAJOR-GENERAL N. P. BANKS.
11. MAJOR-GENERAL B. F. BUTLER.
12. MAJOR-GENERAL DAVID HUNTER.
13. MAJOR-GENERAL E. D. BAKER.
14. MAJOR-GENERAL IRVIN McDOWELL.
15. MAJOR-GENERAL A. E. BURNSIDE.
16. MAJOR-GENERAL DON CARLOS BUELL.
17. MAJOR-GENERAL JOHN POPE.
18. MAJOR-GENERAL SAMUEL R. CURTIS.
19. MAJOR-GENERAL FRANZ SIGEL.
20. MAJOR-GENERAL J. A. McCLERNAND.
21. MAJOR-GENERAL LEWIS WALLACE.
22. MAJOR-GENERAL W. S. ROSECRANS.
23. MAJOR-GENERAL O. M. MITCHEL.
24. MAJOR-GENERAL CASSIUS M. CLAY.
25. MAJOR-GENERAL JESSE L. RENO.
26. MAJOR-GENERAL E. O. C. ORD.
27. MAJOR-GENERAL JOSEPH HOOKER.
28. MAJOR-GENERAL S. P. HEINTZELMAN.
29. MAJOR-GENERAL SILAS CASEY.
30. MAJOR-GENERAL FITZ JOHN PORTER.
31. MAJOR-GENERAL W. B. FRANKLIN.
32. MAJOR-GENERAL PHILIP KEARNEY.
33. MAJOR-GENERAL A. DOUBLEDAY.
34. MAJOR-GENERAL DANIEL BUTTERFIELD.
35. MAJOR-GENERAL I. I. STEVENS.
36. MAJOR-GENERAL CARL SCHURZ.
37. MAJOR-GENERAL J. K. F. MANSFIELD.
38. MAJOR-GENERAL J. A. GARFIELD.
39. MAJOR-GENERAL J. DOLSON COX.
40. MAJOR-GENERAL WILLIAM SPRAGUE.
41. BRIGADIER-GENERAL ROBERT ANDERSON.
42. BRIGADIER-GENERAL NATHANIEL LYON.
43. BRIGADIER-GENERAL GEORGE A. McCALL.
44. BRIGADIER-GENERAL FRED. W. LANDER.
45. BRIGADIER-GENERAL MICHAEL CORCORAN.
46. BRIGADIER-GENERAL LOUIS BLENKER.
47. BRIGADIER-GENERAL JAMES S. WADSWORTH.
48. BRIGADIER-GENERAL EGBERT L. VIELE.
49. BRIGADIER-GENERAL JAMES SHIELDS.
50. BRIGADIER-GENERAL ABRAM DURYEE.
51. BRIGADIER-GENERAL THOMAS F. MEAGHER.
52. BRIGADIER-GENERAL W. H. L. WALLACE.
53. BRIGADIER-GENERAL CUVIER GROVER.
54. BRIGADIER-GENERAL MAX WEBER.
55. BRIGADIER-GENERAL JOSEPH B. CARR.
56. BRIGADIER-GENERAL J. H. HOBART WARD.
57. COLONEL HENRY WILSON.
58. COLONEL RUSH C. HAWKINS.
59. COLONEL E. E. ELLSWORTH.
60. COLONEL JAMES A. MULLIGAN.
61. MAJOR THEODORE WINTHROP.
62. CAPTAIN THOMAS B. HAINES.
63. CAPTAIN JOHN FOOT.
64. REV. ARTHUR B. FULLER, CHAPLAIN.
65. OFFICERS OF OUR NAVY (Group).
66. VICE-ADMIRAL D. G. FARRAGUT.
67. REAR-ADMIRAL S. H. STRINGHAM.
68. REAR-ADMIRAL L. M. GOLDSBOROUGH.
69. REAR-ADMIRAL S. F. DU PONT.
70. REAR-ADMIRAL A. H. FOOTE.
71. REAR-ADMIRAL C. H. DAVIS.
72. REAR-ADMIRAL D. D. PORTER.
73. COMMODORE CHARLES WILKES.
74. COMMANDER JOHN L. WORDEN.
75. S. B. BRITTAN, JR., A. D. C.

Our Army.

LIEUTENANT-GENERAL WINFIELD SCOTT, U.S.A.

> —— " Would thou hadst less deserv'd;
> That the proportion both of thanks and payment
> Might have been mine! only I have left to say,
> More is thy due than more than all can pay."

THIS " hero of a hundred fights," was born near Petersburgh, Virginia, June 13th, 1786. He was educated at the Richmond High School, whence he went to William and Mary College, where he studied law. He was admitted to the bar in 1806, and the next year, removed to South Carolina; but when the Army Enlargement Bill passed Congress, young Scott entered the army as captain of light artillery.

In 1809, Captain Scott was ordered to join the army in Louisiana, commanded by General Wilkinson. The next year, Wilkinson was superceded and Scott openly expressed the opinion that he was implicated in Burr's conspiracy. For this, Captain Scott was court-martialled, and suspended from the army for one year. In July, 1812, he was made a lieutenant-colonel in the second artillery, and stationed at Black Rock, with two companies, with which he covered the passage of the Niagara in the attack on Queenstown, October 13th. Later in the day he was obliged to surrender his whole command as prisoners of war, by the overpowering force of the enemy. He was exchanged in January, 1813, and at the capture of Fort George, Colonel Scott led the assault and was the first to enter it, where he was wounded by a splinter.

In March, 1814, Colonel Scott was made a brigadier-general, and on the 5th of July, decided the battle of Chippewa by a brilliant bayonet charge. For his gallant conduct in this, and the battle of Lundy's Lane, where he was severely wounded, Scott was breveted major-general, presented with a gold medal by Congress, and offered the post of secretary of war, which he declined in favor of General Brown. For the purpose of recovering from his wounds, he travelled in Europe, returning in 1816.

In 1836, he conducted the Seminole campaign, which was " well devised, and prosecuted with energy, steadiness and ability." January 4th, 1838, General Scott was ordered to the Canada frontier, and it was mainly through his exertions that a war with Great Britain was averted. Again it was averted in 1839, by the peaceful settlement of the Maine boundary dispute, by General Scott and Sir John Harvey.

In June, 1841, he became commander-in-chief of the army of the United States, by the death of Major-General Alexander Macomb.

President Polk declared war with Mexico, May 11th, 1846, and on March 12th, 1847,

General Scott invested Vera Cruz, which surrendered to him on the 27th. Thence to Mexico, was one continued series of glorious victories. Cerro Gordo, Jalapa, La Perote, Puebla, Conteras, Churubusco, Chapultepec, and Molinôs del Rey, crowned the victor with laurels; and when on the 14th of September the second conqueror of Mexico, stood within "the halls of the Montezumas," his triumph was complete, and Winfield Scott stood before the world, the foremost general of the age. Peace was concluded February 2d, 1848, and shortly after he was court-martialled upon charges preferred against him by brevet Major-General Worth, but no decision was ever given and General Scott resumed his position as commander-in-chief of the army.

The Whig National Convention, which met at Baltimore in June, 1852, chose him as their candidate for the office of President of the United States, but he was defeated by General Pierce, the Democratic nominee. In 1859, Congress conferred upon him an honor which has been paid to no man else save Washington. He was created Lieutenant-General of the Army of the United States.

Soon after the advent of the rebellion of 1861, the old veteran, pressed down by the infirmities of age, feeling himself unequal to the laborious duties of another campaign, retired from the army. This act elicited from President Lincoln the following order, which was read to General Scott at his residence, by the President, attended by all of his Cabinet:

"On the 1st day of November, A. D. 1861, upon his own application to the President of the United States, brevet Lieutenant-General Winfield Scott is ordered to be placed, and hereby is placed upon the list of retired officers of the army of the United States, without reduction in his current pay, subsistence or allowance.

"The American people will hear with sadness and deep emotion that General Scott has withdrawn from the active control of the army; while the President and unanimous Cabinet express their own and the nation's sympathy in his personal affliction, and their profound sense of important public services rendered by him to his country during his long and brilliant career, among which will be gratefully distinguished his faithful devotion to the Constitution, the Union, and the Flag, when assailed by parricidal rebellion.
"ABRAHAM LINCOLN."

On the same day he was succeeded by Major-General George B. McClellan, who issued an order formally assuming command of the army. Eight days later, General Scott sailed from New York for Europe, to recruit his health, now greatly impaired both in mind and body. On his return, he retired to his family mansion in the City of Elizabeth, N. J., where he remained until June 2d, 1862, when he took his departure for West Point, there to spend the summer months.

In March, 1817, General Scott was married to Miss Maria Mayo, daughter of Mr. John Mayo, of Richmond. Va. By her he has several daughters, but no sons. When he dies, his great name dies with him.

LIEUTENANT-GENERAL U. S. GRANT, U. S. A.

> "In that the scholar's craft, the captain's skill,
> In thee conjoined, work fitting triumphs still;
> And nobler yet the patriotic thrill
> Which guides the master-triumphs of thy will!"

ULYSSES S. GRANT was born at Point Pleasant, Clermont county, Ohio, on the 27th of April, 1822. Entering West Point in 1839, he graduated on the 1st of July, 1843, and, as brevet second-lieutenant, was assigned to the fourth infantry, in which he first saw service on the Rio Grande. At Comargo, in September, 1846, he was appointed regimental quartermaster; and for gallant and meritorious conduct at Palo Alto, Resaca de la Palma, and Monterey, he was promoted to adjutant. Joining Scott's army at Vera Cruz, he participated with great credit in every battle from that place to the city of Mexico. For his gallantry at El Molinos del Rey he was breveted first-lieutenant, September 8th, 1847; and on the 13th, captain, for Chapultepec. In 1852, the fourth infantry was ordered to Oregon, where Lieutenant Grant was soon after promoted to a captaincy. In the following year he resigned his commission, and, after a residence of six years in St. Louis, removed to Galena, Illinois, where he devoted himself to mercantile pursuits until the breaking out of the Great Rebellion of 1861, when Governor Yates appointed him colonel of the twenty-first Illinois volunteers, with which he went into active service in Missouri.

The President appointed him a brigadier-general of volunteers, to date from the 17th of May, and assigned him to the command of the district of Cairo, where his first acts were the seizure of Paducah and the battle of Belmont. Active operations were continued with the co-operation of Flag-Officer Foote, and Fort Henry was captured on the 8th of February, 1862. Leaving it on the 12th, General Grant laid siege to Fort Donelson, and, after a two days' fight, drove the enemy into his inner works on the 15th, after a terrible and bloody conflict. The next morning Buckner unconditionally surrendered, and the President rewarded the victor with the commission of major-general of volunteers, bearing the date of the capitulation.

General Grant then marched to Pittsburg Landing, where he was suddenly attacked while awaiting the arrival of Buell. Though he contested every inch with unsurpassed bravery and stubbornness, the enemy, more than double in numbers, drove him back nearly to the river, when he brought them to a stand by the skilful disposition of his batteries and the gunboats. Buell arriving in the night, Grant attacked the enemy in the morning, and drove them back to their intrenchments with great slaughter. General Halleck soon after arrived and assumed command, but upon being ordered to

LIEUTENANT-GENERAL U. S. GRANT, U. S. A.

Washington as General-in-Chief, Grant was replaced in command of the Department of the Tennessee, including Rosecrans' corps.

After Sherman's gallant but unsuccessful attack on Vicksburg, on the 28th and 29th of December, many plans were attempted in vain to take that city in the rear. At length, in the latter part of April, 1863, successfully running his fleet past the batteries in the night, and marching his troops about seventy miles down the Mississippi, he crossed the river at Bruinsburg on the 30th, and, turning Grand Gulf, defeated the enemy with heavy loss at Port Gibson and Fourteen-mile Creek, on the 1st and 3d of May. Rapidly marching north, he fought the battles of Raymond on the 12th, Jackson on the 14th, Champion's Hill on the 16th, and Big Black River Bridge on the 17th,—in all of which he was gloriously victorious. On the 19th he carried the rifle-pits to the north of the city, and completely surrounded it. Another terrific but unsuccessful assault was made on the 22d; and, on the 29th, a heavy bombardment was opened, which, continuing almost without intermission during the following month, accompanied by McPherson's skilful sapping and mining, compelled Pemberton, on the afternoon of July 3d, to surrender to General Grant, who occupied the city on the following day.

Shortly after the fall of Vicksburg, General Grant was commissioned a major-general in the regular army, *vice* General Wool, retired.

At Louisville, on the 18th of October, by order of the President, General Grant assumed command of the Military Division of the Mississippi, embracing the Departments of the Tennessee, Cumberland, and Ohio. Repairing at once to Chattanooga, he brought up Hooker's command, and, throwing General W. F. Smith across the river, recaptured the points of Lookout Mountain commanding it, on the 27th, 28th, and 29th of October. This very important success having been obtained, General Grant prepared to advance upon the enemy in force, and Thomas opened the great battle of Chattanooga on the 23d of November. On the 24th the battle was renewed along the entire line, and on the 25th the whole of Missionary Ridge to the Chickamauga was gallantly carried, and the enemy completely routed. Considering the great strength of the rebel position and the difficulty of storming his intrenchments, this must be regarded as one of the most remarkable battles in history, and too much praise can scarcely be awarded to the skilful commander, or to his brave and gallant troops.

The unexampled services of General Grant demanded an appropriate reward, and were themselves demanded by the people, in a higher sphere. Congress accordingly recreated the grade of lieutenant-general, and on the 9th of March, 1864, the President presented him with a commission of that rank, and on the 11th assigned him to the supreme command of all the armies of the United States. To continue our biography of General Grant would be to give a complete history of our military operations from that time forward, which our brief space precludes, and for which we refer the reader to our sketches of his subordinate commanders.

Geo. B. McClellan

MAJOR-GENERAL GEORGE B. McCLELLAN, U.S.A.

*———"All tongues speak of him,
And the bleared sights are spectacled to see him."*

GEORGE BRINTON MCCLELLAN is the son of an eminent physician of Philadelphia, where he was born on the 3d of December, 1826. He graduated at West Point in 1846, and on the 1st of July was commissioned a second-lieutenant of engineers. His company sailed from West Point, September 24th, under command of Captain Swift. They went first to Comargo, whence they were ordered to Matamoras, Tampico, and finally Vera Cruz, where, until the surrender of the castle, Lieutenant McClellan was engaged in the most severe duties, which were executed "with unsurpassed intelligence and zeal." At Conteras he had his horse shot under him by the Mexican pickets. General Twiggs, in his official report, says "Lieutenant George B. McClellan, after Lieutenant Calendar was wounded, took charge of and managed the howitzer battery with judgment and success, until it became so disabled as to require shelter. For Lieutenant McClellan's efficiency in this affair, I present his name for the favorable consideration of the general-in-chief." For "gallant and meritorious conduct in the battles of Conteras and Churubusco," he was breveted first-lieutenant; and "for gallant and meritorious conduct in the battle of Molino del Rey," captain; but the latter brevet he declined to accept. In the battle of Chepultepec he won the admiration of all about him; and for his gallant conduct on that day he was breveted captain.

Captain McClellan returned in June, 1847. Between 1848 and 1851 he translated from the French a manual of bayonet exercise which has become the text-book of the army. In 1851, he superintended the construction of Fort Delaware, and in 1852 he explored the Red River under Captain Marcy, and served as senior engineer on the staff of General P. F. Smith. In 1853, Captain McClellan was employed on the survey to ascertain the best route for a railroad between the Mississippi and the Pacific, also in the exploration of the forty-seventh and forty-ninth parallels of north latitude.

After executing a secret service commission in the West Indies, he received, in 1855, a captaincy in the first United States cavalry. In April, of the same year, he sailed for Europe and proceeded to the Crimea and to northern Russia to observe the operations of the war then in progress; and afterwards visited the principal military establishments in Europe. His report "On the Organization of European Armies, and the Operations of the War," is considered a most valuable work.

Captain McClellan resigned his position in the army, January 16th, 1857, to accept that of vice-president and chief engineer of the Illinois Central Railroad, and after

MAJOR-GENERAL GEORGE B. McCLELLAN, U.S.A.

three years upon that road he became general superintendent of the Ohio and Mississippi line. He held this position when the rebellion broke out.

When President Lincoln issued his proclamation calling for 75,000 men, the young ex-captain was chosen by Ohio as the best qualified to organize her volunteer regiments into an army. In assembling her forces and placing them upon an efficient war footing, he showed so much of that determination and originality which had characterized his services in Mexico, that on the 14th of May, 1861, he was appointed a major-general in the army of the United States, and assigned to the command of the Department of the Ohio.

On the 20th of June, he arrived at Phillipi, and assumed command of the Federal forces in Western Virginia.

On the 10th of July, he attacked Colonel Pegram at Rich Mountain, and the next day sent General Rosecrans with about 4,000 men to take the small fort on the hill-top, and attack the main one in the rear, which he accomplished after a severe march of eight miles; but the rebels in the lower fort no sooner heard that the upper one was taken, than they fled in all directions, leaving their arms, ammunition, etc., together with many prisoners, in the hands of the victor, who by a rapid march occupied Beverly. Two days later, Colonel Pegram surrendered his whole command, unconditionally, to General McClellan.

General Morris was immediately dispatched in pursuit of Garnett. Garnett made a stand at Carrick's ford, on the Cheat River, where he was killed, his army disorganized, and all his baggage captured. Thus by a series of brilliant movements, Western Virginia was freed of the armed rabble that had overrun it, in only twenty-four days after General McClellan assumed the command. In recognition of this first considerable success of the war, Congress, on the 16th of July, passed a joint resolution of thanks to General McClellan and the officers and soldiers under his command.

Soon after the disastrous battle of Bull Run, General McClellan was ordered to Washington to take command of the fresh troops that poured in from every loyal state. He arrived at the Capital on the 25th of July, and at once infused his own energy into every department. On the 3d of August, his appointment as a major-general was confirmed by the Senate; and on the 20th, by general order, he assumed command of the army of the Potomac. Lieutenant-General Scott retired from active service on the 1st of November, 1861, and General McClellan, being next in rank, succeeded him on the same day. On the 11th of March, 1862, he took the field for active operations at the head of the army of the Potomac, and by special order of the President was relieved from the command of the other departments.

MAJOR-GENERAL JOHN C. FREMONT, U.S.A.

"Thank God! that while the hour is struck, we have the living Man
To bear our eagle banner against the spoiler's van,
Strong hand to wield the wavering helm, warm heart and coolest brain,
Heroic Sage, wise Hero—a crowned soul again!'"

JOHN CHARLES FREMONT was born in Savannah, Ga., January 21, 1813. At the age of fifteen he entered Charleston College, where he became conspicuous for his remarkable attainments in mathematics. In 1833, he obtained the position of teacher of mathematics on board of the United States sloop-of-war Natchez. He was absent for more than two years, and on his return to Charleston received the degree of bachelor and master of arts. Shortly afterwards he passed successfully a vigorous examination at Baltimore, for the post of professor of mathematics in the navy, and was appointed to the frigate Independence; but he soon resolved to quit the sea, and engaged himself as a surveyor and railroad engineer on a line between Charleston, S. C., and Augusta, Ga. Subsequently he assisted in the survey of the railroad line from Charleston to Cincinnati, and particularly in the exploration of the mountain passes between South Carolina and Tennessee. He was engaged in this work until the autumn of 1837, when he accompanied Captain Williams, of the United States Army, on a military reconnoissance of the mountainous Cherokee country in Georgia, North Carolina, and Tennessee. In anticipation of hostilities with the Indians, this survey was rapidly made in the depth of winter, and was his (Fremont's) first experience of a campaign amid mountain snows.

In 1838–9, he accompanied M. Nicollet, a distinguished man of science, in explorations of the country between the Missouri and the British line. These explorations were made under the authority of the government, and while engaged in them, in 1838, he received from President Van Buren, under date of July 7, a commission as second-lieutenant in the corps of topographical engineers. He subsequently made an examination of the River Des Moines, upon the Western frontier. The survey was rapidly executed, and shortly after he returned from this duty, he married Jessie, daughter of Colonel Thomas H. Benton, Senator from Missouri, Oct. 19th, 1841.

In the following year he made a geographical survey of the entire territory of the United States from the Missouri River to the Pacific Ocean, the feasibility of an overland communication being a leading idea in his scheme of explorations.

In 1845, he made an exploration of the great basin and mountain region of Oregon and California, and also of the Sierra Nevada.

MAJOR-GENERAL JOHN C. FREMONT, U.S.A.

He was appointed lieutenant-colonel in the regiment of mounted riflemen, May 27, 1846. He took an active part during the war with Mexico, and commanded a battalion of California volunteers, from July to November, 1846. During the war, he had a misunderstanding with General Kearney, and on his return to Washington was tried by a court martial, and through the influence of the West Point faction, was found guilty of insubordination but recommended to the clemency of the President. He refused to accept the recommendation of the court, and left the army.

In 1848, he started on a fourth expedition to the Rocky Mountains at his own expense, and after a tedious journey reached Sacramento in 1849. Here he determined to settle, having, in 1847, purchased the Maraposa estate.

In March, 1849, after his retirement from the army, he was appointed one of the United States commissioners to run the boundary line between the United States and Mexico, and relinquished the post on being elected a United States Senator from California. In 1850, while in the Senate, Baron Humboldt, in behalf of the King of Prussia, sent him the golden medal for "proficiency in the sciences." He was subsequently made an honorary member in the royal geographical societies of Berlin and London.

In September, 1853, he made a fifth expedition from the Mississippi valley to the Pacific, and in 1856 he took up his residence in New York city, for the purpose of preparing for publication the narrative of his last expedition. In June, 1856, he was nominated for the Presidency of the United States by the Republican National Convention, and at the election in November following, received 114 electoral votes.

His subsequent career is too fresh in the public mind to need mention here. It is a well known fact that Fremont has ever had the tremendous influence of the West Point faction to contend against, and that in all his triumphs he is, therefore, doubly victorious. His appointment and speedy confirmation as major-general in the army of the United States, was peculiarly mortifying to his enemies, and the West Point and pro-slavery influences banded together to overthrow him. We all know how he was hampered and persecuted in Missouri; Adjutant-General Thomas' "report" served but to show the nobleness of the general and the baseness of his enemies. But at last, on the eve of a grand battle, he was removed in a manner more discreditable to the government than to its victim.

But Fremont was enshrined in the hearts of the people and he could not be neglected. He was therefore assigned to the command of the "Mountain Department," where he acquitted himself nobly. But his popularity was again getting too great; his despicable enemies again prevailed, and the noble commander was forced to resign. But the end is not yet. John C. Fremont is preëminently a man of the people, and by them he will never be forgotten.

MAJOR-GENERAL HENRY W. HALLECK, U.S.A.

> "Proud was his tone, but calm; his eye
> Had that compelling dignity,
> His mien that bearing, haught and high,
> Which common spirits fear."

HENRY WAGER HALLECK is a son of the Honorable Joseph Halleck, and was born in the year 1820, at Weston, Oneida county, New York. After an education at the Hudson Academy, he entered the West Point Military Academy in 1835. He graduated in 1839, standing third in his class, and was breveted second-lieutenant of engineers on the 1st of July. From that time to June, 1840, he served there as assistant professor of engineering. In 1841 he published his first work, "Bitumen and its Uses." In 1845, Lieutenant Halleck delivered a course of lectures in Boston on "Military Science and Art," which he collected in one volume in 1846, and prefixed an essay on the "Justifiableness of War."

In 1845 he was commissioned first-lieutenant, and ordered to Lower California, where he served through the Mexican War. He was breveted captain for "gallant and meritorious conduct" in the affairs with the enemy on the 19th and 20th of November, 1847. During the military governments of Kearney, Mason, and Riley, from 1847 to the close of 1849, he was secretary of state of the Territory of California. He was chief of Commodore Shubrick's staff during 1847 and 1848, and in 1849 was a member of the convention to form, and of the committee to draft, the Constitution of the State of California. In July, 1853, he was promoted to a full captaincy of engineers; but he was already identified with the interests of the Golden State, and he finally resigned his position in the army on the 1st of August, 1854.

Perfecting his legal studies, he soon became a leading member of the San Francisco bar; and the name of "Halleck, Billings & Co." became synonymous with victory in the legal battles in the California courts.

The breaking out of the great Southern rebellion found Halleck enjoying a lucrative practice. He, however, closed his business and offered his services to the War Department. On the recommendation of Lieutenant-General Scott, the President appointed him a major-general of the regular army of the United States on the 19th of August, 1861, and the Senate confirmed the appointment February 10th, 1862.

On the 2d of November, 1861, General Fremont was removed from the command of the Department of the West, and Halleck was appointed his successor. He arrived at Saint Louis on the 18th, and formally took command of the department on the following day. On the 20th he issued his celebrated Order No. 3, excluding fugitive slaves from his lines. On the 4th of December, General Halleck issued an order quartering the Union refugees upon avowed secessionists, charging the expense of their board to them, on the ground that, although they had not themselves plundered and driven forth those unfortunate people, they were giving aid and comfort to those who had. This order had a salutary effect, and cooled the ardor of the wealthy traitors of Saint Louis. On the 22d of the same month another order was issued, in which the hanging of bridge-burners was ordered.

On the 6th and 7th of April, 1862, was fought the great battle of Shiloh, which demonstrated that Beauregard was strongly intrenched at Corinth with a considerable force. Halleck soon arrived at Pittsburg, and, ordering Pope to join him, laid siege to Corinth. Some of his officers repeatedly asked permission to "walk right into Corinth;" but Halleck, resolving not to incur even the hazard of a defeat, allowed no advances beyond the gradual closing of his lines. The grand assault was ordered on the morning of May 30th, and the Federal divisions leaped over the intrenchments to find the enemy gone.

In the midst of his operations in Tennessee, General Halleck was summoned to Washington by the following order of the President, dated July 11th, 1862: "Ordered, that Major-General Henry W. Halleck be assigned to the command of the whole land forces of the United States as general-in-chief, and that he repair to this capital as soon as he can with safety to the positions and operations within the department now under his special charge."

Disposing of his command to Grant and Buell, he hastened to Washington, where he arrived on the 22d of July. Consultations were had with the President, cabinet, and generals; the Peninsula was visited; Pope was advanced toward Richmond, and McClellan drawn from the Peninsula. On the 7th of November, 1862, at the request of General Halleck, McClellan was removed from the command of the army of the Potomac, and Burnside assigned to it. On the 30th of the same month, he made his official report—a document of great ability and worth.

As a statesman, his place would be administration; as a soldier, organizing and planning; as a lawyer, that of an astute and subtle counsellor.

MAJOR-GENERAL JOHN E. WOOL, U.S.A.

> "I am one,
> Who finds within me a nobility
> That spurns the idle pratings of the great,
> And their mean boast of what their fathers were,
> While they themselves are fools effeminate,
> The scorn of all who know the worth of mind
> And virtue."

JOHN ELLIS WOOL was born at Newburgh, New York, in the year 1789. He received only a rudimentary education, and for many years was a clerk in a store at Troy, but being dissatisfied with his occupation, he renounced it and began the study of law. Upon the enlargement of the army he obtained, April 14th, 1812, a captain's commission in the thirteenth regiment of infantry, and soon after joined General Van Rensselaer, on the Niagara frontier, and in the expedition against Queenstown the young captain won great distinction. After Colonel Van Rensselaer was carried from the field, the command devolved upon Captains Wool and Ogilvie until the arrival of General Van Rensselaer. Wool received a severe wound in this battle, and by the eventual surrender became a prisoner of war. He was promoted to a majority, and upon his exchange, assigned to the twenty-ninth regiment of infantry, April 13th, 1813. Major Wool again became conspicuous for his gallantry in the repulse of General Provost at Plattsburg, and for his bravery, was breveted lieutenant-colonel.

In September, 1816, he was appointed inspector-general of the army, with the rank of colonel; in February, 1818, lieutenant-colonel of infantry; and "for ten years of faithful service" he was breveted brigadier-general, April 29th, 1826. In 1832, he travelled in Europe on a government commission, and was present at the siege of Antwerp. He was appointed a full brigadier-general, June 25th, 1841.

In the Mexican War, General Wool commanded the "centre division," organized to act against Chihuahua. He left San Antonio de Bexar with three thousand men, September 26th, 1846, and in eleven days reached the Rio Grande, near Presido. From Presido he marched by way of San Juan de Nava, San Fernando de Rosas, and Santa Rosa to Monclova. The authorities of the latter place protested against General Wool's advance, but he entered and took formal possession of the town on the 3d of November. On the 24th he took up the line of march for Parras, one hundred and eighty miles distant, where, upon his arrival he was held to coöperate if necessary with General Taylor. He was soon ordered, however to relieve Saltillo, which was threatened by a large force of Mexicans. He marched toward Saltillo, pushing his artillery and cavalry at the rate of forty miles a day. Taylor, Butler and Twiggs hurried forward, and the Mexicans retreated without making an attack. From this time forward his division was merged in the "army of occupation." General Wool joined General Taylor at Agua Nueva, December 21st, 1846. Wool had the honor of choosing the field of battle at Buena Vista, where with but four thousand two hundred men, he held Santa Anna's army of twenty thousand in check until General Taylor came up and assumed the command. For "gallant and meritorious conduct" in this battle, he was breveted major-general in May, 1848.

Upon the close of the Mexican War, General Wool was assigned to the command of the Eastern Military Department of the United States, which position he occupied when the rebellion broke out. He strongly urged the support of Major Anderson in Fort Sumter, and as early as December, 1860, declared that the surrender of that post would put two hundred thousand men in arms in defence of the government.

Through the influence of the West Point and pro-slavery faction at Washington, the veteran was kept in virtual retirement at Troy, at the time of the country's greatest need for experienced and able officers; and assured him that it was done "for the benefit of his health," though he publicly declared that his health had never been better. Great dissatisfaction with the course of the government in this matter, was expressed through the newspapers and otherwise, and at length, August 12th, 1861, he received orders to proceed to Fortress Monroe, and take command of the forces there. He arrived there on the 17th, and at once assumed the command. The forces were made up mostly of volunteers, and had, since the war began, been under the command of Major-General Butler. General Wool immediately instituted a more perfect and thorough discipline, and rapidly fitted the men in his command for any emergency.

He organized a movement against Norfolk, on the 9th of May, 1862. The next morning the troops were landed at Ocean View, and commenced their march toward the city, a short distance from which they were met by the mayor and a deputation of the common council, who surrendered the city to General Wool. The rebel troops fled on their approach, after firing the navy yard and the vessels there, and blowing up the dry dock. After entering the city and formally taking possession of it, he appointed Brigadier-General Egbert L. Viélé Military Governor, and returned to Fortress Monroe.

May 16th, the President appointed him a full major-general of the United States Army, and the appointment was promptly confirmed by the Senate; a tardy recognition of his great and valuable services. For a long time General Wool repeatedly requested that he be given some command not under McClellan, whom he felt to be greatly his inferior; but the government disregarded his request, until, on his positively declining to serve any longer under General McClellan, he was ordered to relieve General Dix, in command of the Department of Annapolis.

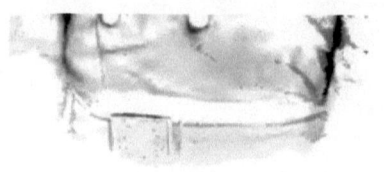

John A. Dix

MAJOR-GENERAL JOHN A. DIX, U.S.V.

"If any one attempts to haul down the American flag, shoot him on the spot."

JOHN ADAMS DIX, son of Lieutenant-Colonel Timothy Dix, U. S. A., was born at Boscawen, New Hampshire, on the 24th of July, 1798. At a very early age he was sent to the academy at Salisbury, and afterwards to Exeter. In 1811, he was transferred to a college at Montreal, under the direction of the Fathers of the Sulpician Order; but in July, 1812, he was compelled to return, in consequence of the opening of hostilities. In December, 1812, young Dix was appointed a cadet in the army of the United States, and was ordered to Baltimore, where his father was then in command.

In March, 1813, the Secretary of War offered him, without solicitation, the choice of a scholarship in the military academy at West Point, or an ensigncy in the army which was then about to take the field. He selected the latter, entered the Fourteenth Infantry, of which his father was then lieutenant-colonel, and immediately marched with his company to Sackett's Harbor. In June, he was appointed adjutant of a battalion, commanded by Major Upham, with which he descended the St. Lawrence, and participated in the perils and hardships of that unfortunate expedition. In November, of the same year, the father of Lieutenant Dix died in camp, leaving his affairs hopelessly disordered, and the son was thrown upon the world with no other means of support than his lieutenant's commission.

In August, 1814, he was transferred to Colonel Wallach's regiment of artillery, and under the guidance of that gallant officer he continued several years, pursuing his studies, whenever his duties enabled him to do so. In 1819, he was appointed an aide-de-camp of General Brown, and in 1825, he was promoted to a captaincy in the Third Artillery, but his health becoming impaired, he obtained leave of absence and travelled through Europe and the West Indies. In 1826, Captain Dix married Miss Catherine Morgan, and two years later, he retired from the army and established himself in Cooperstown, New York, in the practice of law. He soon became one of the most active and influential members of the Democratic party in the State, and in 1830, Governor Throop appointed him Adjutant-General of the State, a post of duty which he filled with honor to himself and advantage to the militia of the State.

In January, 1833, he was chosen Secretary of State of New York, and rendered very efficient services to the State. Mr. Dix was elected a member of the assembly, in 1841, and took a very prominent part in its proceedings. In January, 1845, he was elected a Senator in the Congress of the United States. He was among the most

MAJOR-GENERAL JOHN A. DIX, U.S.V.

useful members of that distinguished body, and took a decided and leading position against the extension of slavery. After his defeat for the governorship of New York, he retired to private life. In 1853, he was appointed Assistant-Treasurer of the United States; but becoming dissatisfied with the official conduct of President Pierce, he resigned his office. Mr. Dix was appointed postmaster of the city of New York, in May, 1860; and on the 11th of January, 1861, he succeeded Mr. Thomas as Secretary of the Treasury, and in this capacity showed great tact, energy, and promptness.

On the 6th of March, 1861, Mr. Dix retired from the Treasury Department; and on the 20th of April, when the assault on Fort Sumter aroused the outraged North, he presided over the immense meeting of the citizens of New York in Union Square, which had been convened to take measures for the defence of the constitution and the enforcement of the laws. As chairman of the Union Defence Committee he was one of the most active and intelligent of its members.

On the 6th of May, he was appointed a major-general in the volunteer force of New York; and on the 14th of June, the President appointed him to a similar position in the volunteer service of the United States, and his appointment was confirmed on the 3d of August. On the 20th of July, he was appointed commander of the department of Maryland, with head-quarters at Baltimore. Under his directions, General Lockwood's expedition to the county of Accomac, in Virginia, was organized and successfully prosecuted; and his energetic and vigilant action was displayed in the complete quiet which prevailed throughout his department. In May, 1862, he was transferred to the command of the military department of Eastern Virginia, with head-quarters at Fortress Monroe.

General Dix possesses great energy of character; and he has always discharged the various duties to which he has been called, with honor to himself and advantage to the country.

MAJOR-GENERAL NATHANIEL P. BANKS, U.S.V.

> "The king hath happily receiv'd, Macbeth,
> The news of thy success; and when he reads
> Thy personal venture in the rebels' fight,
> His wonders and his praises do contend,
> Which should be thine or his."

NATHANIEL PRENTISS BANKS was born in Waltham, Mass., January 30th, 1816. He was the son of an overseer in a cotton factory, and when he was old enough, he himself became a bobbin-boy under the superintendence of his father. Being of a studious disposition, however, all his hours "not occupied in the factory were devoted to the grave and important studies of history, political economy, and the science of government." He soon left the factory and learned the machinist's trade, then became a lecturer, and finally edited the village paper at Waltham, and afterwards at Lowell, in which he earnestly advocated the principles of the Democratic party. After the election of Mr. Polk, he received an office in the Boston Custom House. Waltham was a town of strong Whig proclivities, and despite the reputation of Mr. Banks, he was defeated for six consecutive years, as a candidate for the Massachusetts House of Representatives. On the seventh year, 1848, he was elected, and made his first speech on the 23d of February, 1849, on the extension of slavery. It was a speech worthy of the man and of the old "Bay State," and Mr. Banks became at once the leader of the Democratic party in Massachusetts. In 1850, he was simultaneously elected to both the Senate and the House, but chose the House, where he was elected Speaker; which position he held for two successive sessions.

In 1852, Mr. Banks was elected to Congress by the combined Democrats and Americans. In 1853, he was chosen President of the Convention to revise the Constitution of Massachusetts. He was twice reëlected to the House of Representatives, where he took strong ground against the aggressions of slavery, and argued ably against the "Kansas-Nebraska" Bill.

On the 24th of December, 1856, Mr. Banks resigned his seat in the House, on being elected Governor of his native State, to which position he was reëlected in 1857 and 1858. Declining the nomination for a fourth term, he abandoned the field of politics and removed to Illinois, where he accepted the Presidency of the Illinois Central Railroad.

On the 30th of May, 1861, the President appointed him a Major-General in the volunteer force of the United States, and his appointment was confirmed by the Senate on the 3d of August.

MAJOR-GENERAL NATHANIEL P. BANKS, U.S.V.

General Banks was ordered to take command of the department of Annapolis, with headquarters at Baltimore, on the 10th of June, 1861. The police of that city, though ostensibly its guardians, were really an organized band of armed traitors, ready at any moment to overthrow the federal authorities and compel the State to revolt. All loyal men were gratified, therefore, by the arrest of George P. Kane, the marshal of police, on the morning of June 27th, and his imprisonment in Fort McHenry. On the same day the energetic commander issued a proclamation superceding Marshal Kane and the Board of Police, and appointing Colonel J. R. Kenly, Provost Marshal of the city. The Board of Police continuing their sessions and holding subject to their order the whole police force, General Banks arrested them on the 1st of July, and on examining their headquarters, found it to resemble "in some respects a concealed arsenal."

On the 19th of July, 1861, General Banks was ordered to take command of the Shenandoah. He reached Harper's Ferry and took command on the 25th, and immediately began the work of disciplining and perfecting the organization of his troops.

By the President's War Order of March 9th, 1862, General Banks was put in command of the fifth corps d'armée, and three days after, he commenced his march and occupied Winchester, where his advance under General Shields was attacked by Jackson on the evening of the 22d of March. There being no signs of the enemy the next morning, General Banks left for Washington. About noon, however, the enemy opened the battle, and though the rebels fought desperately, they were compelled to retreat with great loss. General Banks, hearing of the battle, rejoined Shields on the 24th, and at once ordered a pursuit. He arrived at Woodstock on the 1st of April after a sharp running fight with Jackson's rear guard and Ashby's cavalry.

The army under General Banks had been drawn upon to reinforce Generals McClellan and McDowell, until he had but 6,000 men to oppose to the swelled ranks of Jackson's army, numbering 20,000. General Banks' position grew more critical daily, and when on the 23d of May, Colonel Kenly was surprised and defeated at Front Royal, he fell back to Winchester, where he was attacked on the morning of the 25th. After a terrible fight of four hours against such overwhelming numbers, General Banks gave the order to retreat. He crossed the Potomac in safety at Williamsport, with all his train, after a running battle of 65 miles in two days. General Sigel expressed great admiration of the skill, promptitude and coolness with which it was conducted, and pronounced it the most masterly retreat on record. General Banks being reinforced, pursued in his turn, the flying Jackson, and occupied Front Royal on the 30th of May, and Martinsburg on the 31st.

By special order of the President, June 26th, 1862, the armies of Generals Fremont, Banks, and McDowell, were formed into three corps d'armée, commanded by their respective generals, the whole to be called the army of Virginia, to be commanded by General Pope.

MAJOR-GENERAL BENJAMIN F. BUTLER, U.S.V.

> "Un magistrat intégre et un brave officier, sont également estimables ; celui-là fait la guerre aux ennemis domestiques, celui-ci nous protège contre les ennemis extérieurs."

BENJAMIN FRANKLIN BUTLER was born in Deerfield, Rockingham county, New Hampshire, on the 5th of November, 1818, and began his education at the Lowell High School. Fitting himself for college at the Exeter Academy, he entered Waterville College, Maine, where he graduated with honors. He studied law in the office of William Smith, of Lowell, and was admitted to the bar in 1846. Plunging into law and politics, he pursued both with equal ardor, and displayed that adroitness and energy which have always characterized him. His great fertility in expedients, and success in defending awkward suits, soon won him the reputation of being the ablest criminal lawyer in the State. In 1853, Mr. Butler was elected to the House; and in 1858, to the Senate of the State. In 1860 he was a very prominent delegate to the Charleston and Baltimore conventions.

In 1857 he was appointed a brigadier-general of the State militia, which position he held when the great slaveholders' rebellion broke out. The hour was approaching when his alert brain and strong hand were to be worth untold gold—and none knew it so well as he. On the issue of the President's proclamation, calling for volunteers, General Butler saw the opportunity afforded for military distinction, and eagerly availed himself of it. He offered his services to Governor Andrew; they were accepted, and with a single regiment he marched into Maryland, seized the "Constitution," descended upon Annapolis, and held it. The Department of Annapolis was created, including Baltimore, and Butler was put in command and appointed a major-general in the volunteer force of the United States on the 16th of May, 1861. General Butler strengthened his exposed position, and set his soldiers to constructing locomotives, building bridges, and making railroads. On the 8th of May he took possession of the Relay House, and fortified himself there, controlling the channel of communication between the traitors of Baltimore and Harper's Ferry. On the 13th he marched into Baltimore with but two regiments and a battery; intrenched himself on Federal Hill, overlooking the city; issued his proclamation of protection to all loyalists; arrested traitors; seized arms and munitions of war; and rode through the perilous streets at the head of a single company of the Massachusetts Sixth, which the mob had assaulted but three weeks before. Baltimore had found its master.

On the 20th of May, General Butler was assigned to the command of the Department of Virginia, with headquarters at Fortress Monroe. While there, the disastrous affair of Big Bethel occurred, and he was superseded by General Wool, August 12th.

On the 1st of September, the War Department " authorized Major-General B. F. Butler to raise, organize, arm, uniform and equip a volunteer force for the war, in the New England States, not exceeding six regiments." Two days later, the War Department authorized him " to fit out and prepare such troops in New England as he may judge fit for the purpose, to make an expedition along the eastern shore of Virginia," etc. At length, on the 20th of February, 1862, General Butler left Boston for Ship Island, in Mississippi Sound, where he arrived on the 23d of March, with fifteen thousand men, to operate against New Orleans. He left Ship Island on the 17th of April, with twenty-five hundred men; steamed up the Mississippi, and after the bombardment of Forts Jackson and St. Philip, proceeded to New Orleans, where he arrived on the 28th, and took up his quarters in the St. Charles Hotel. He was received with sullen silence by the people, whom he was to bring into order and submission by his iron will and tireless energy.

Here General Butler again loomed up as the man for the hour. His executive ability, his ready wit, decision, unflinching justice, and, in short, all the peculiar powers of his mind, came into play. No man could have done better, few so well. His course was, from the first, necessarily a stringent one. He suppressed "The Delta" and "The Bee," for advocating destruction of produce; arrested several British subjects, for " giving aid and comfort to the enemy;" seized a large amount of specie belonging to the rebels, in the office of the consul for the Netherlands; stopped the circulation of confederate paper money; distributed among the suffering poor the provisions intended for the support of the Southern army; levied a tax on rebel sympathizers; gave care and protection to Mrs. Beauregard, whom he found in the house of Mr. Slidell; reëstablished courts of justice; compelled the government of the city to clean it, against their will; and issued that celebrated and characteristic proclamation respecting active female traitors, which at once extirpated a most annoying nuisance. He found the city demoralized; he shaped order out of chaos. He has been a faithful servant of the Government, and his services will link his name forever with that of the Crescent City.

MAJOR-GENERAL D. HUNTER, U.S.V.

"Proclaim liberty throughout all the land, unto all the inhabitants thereof."

DAVID HUNTER was born in the city of Washington, District of Columbia, on the 21st of July, 1802. Entering the West Point Military Academy at the age of sixteen, he graduated in 1822, the twenty-fifth in rank in a class of forty, and on the 1st of July received the appointment of second-lieutenant in the Fifth Regiment of United States Infantry. In 1828, he was promoted to the rank of first-lieutenant, and in 1833 to a captaincy in the first dragoons, in which capacity he twice crossed the plains to the Rocky Mountains. He resigned his position in the army in 1836, and entered the forwarding business in Chicago. He, however, returned to the army in 1841 as paymaster, with the rank of major, which rank he held at the time of the breaking out of the great rebellion in 1861.

Major Hunter was one of the four officers detailed by the War Department to escort the newly-elected President from Springfield to Washington; but at Buffalo, owing to the pressure of the crowd, he suffered a dislocation of the collar bone. Shortly after, May 14th, 1861, he was commissioned colonel of the Sixth United States Cavalry. At the battle of Bull Run he commanded the second division, but was severely wounded in the neck early in the action, and compelled to return to Washington. His division fought well, and did good service on that bloody field.

On the 3d of August, 1861, Colonel Hunter was appointed a brigadier-general of volunteers, his commission to bear date May 17th, 1861; and on the 13th of August he was made a major-general of volunteers, and sent to Missouri as second in command. On the 27th of October, General Fremont arrived at Springfield, and was preparing to attack Price, when, on the 2d of November, he received a peremptory order to turn over the command to General Hunter, who arrived on the following day and formally assumed the command. At a council of war held that evening it was resolved to attack the enemy on the following morning; but General Hunter, by command of the President, fell back on Saint Louis, and Southern Missouri was again overrun by the rebel marauders.

On the 19th of November, 1861, General Halleck formally assumed command of the Western Department, and General Hunter was assigned to the Department of Kansas, where he remained until March, 1862. On the 15th of that month he was ordered to the Department of the South, with headquarters at Beaufort, South Carolina. He arrived there on the 30th, and immediately assumed command

MAJOR-GENERAL D. HUNTER, U. S. V.

One of his first and most important acts was the following brief and pithy order, generally known as "Hunter's Emancipation Proclamation:"

"HEADQUARTERS, DEPARTMENT OF THE SOUTH, HILTON HEAD, S. C., May 9, 1862.
"GENERAL ORDERS, No. 11.

"The three States of Georgia, Florida, and South Carolina, comprising the Military Department of the South, having deliberately declared themselves no longer under the protection of the United States of America, and having taken up arms against the said United States, it became a military necessity to declare them under martial law. This was accordingly done on the 25th day of April, 1862. Slavery and martial law in a free country are altogether incompatible. The persons in these three States, Georgia, Florida, and South Carolina, heretofore held as slaves, are therefore declared forever free.

[Official.] "DAVID HUNTER, Major-General Commanding.
"ED. W. SMITH, Acting Assistant Adjutant-General."

General Hunter having indubitable evidence that the rebels had impressed, armed, and drilled the slaves to fight against us, this order was clearly a military necessity. But he did not stop here. Believing, like Napoleon, that it is not unlawful to learn a lesson from the enemy, and that in war a general should use all means at his command against his foe, he also organized a negro brigade, and detailed officers to train them to the use of arms. Both willing and able, they soon attained considerable proficiency, and under the wise administration of General Saxton, did good service in the cause of liberty.

This order struck at the very foundation and support of the rebellion, and made dire consternation among the rebels. The rebel Congress at Richmond immediately passed resolutions to hang Generals Hunter and Phelps, who had issued a similar order, if captured, instead of treating them as prisoners of war. Under a mistaken policy, which was afterwards abandoned, the President annulled General Hunter's order on the 19th of May, 1862, and compelled General Phelps to resign and come home.

But though annulled, the order was a great fact. It indicated progress. It pointed the way to unity and victory. Revolutions take no backward steps till their full circle is accomplished. And this infernal rebellion, fomented and inaugurated in the interest of slavery, and designed to insure to that great wrong boundless aggrandizement, security and sway, is destined, in the Providence of God, to work its utter downfall and ruin.

In September, 1862, General Hunter was ordered to Washington to act as president of a court of inquiry on the surrender of Harper's Ferry, McClellan's Maryland campaign, etc., and as president of a number of courts-martial. On the decease of Major-General Mitchel, November 30th, 1862, General Hunter was reappointed to the command of the department of the South, but was retained in Washington by the above-mentioned court.

MAJOR-GENERAL E. D. BAKER, U. S. V.

> "Then, my own, the Senate's honor,
> Western Lands, and Key-Stone State,
> Tell to me a general's duty
> Is to dare a soldier's fate."

THE subject of this sketch, though of foreign birth, has become one of the martyrs of our liberty by laying down his life so nobly in its defence. Struggling nobly against poverty in his early life, the poor weaver became one of the greatest statesmen, one of the bravest soldiers, one of the truest patriots that our free institutions have yet developed. Crossing the Alleghanies on foot, and passing down the Wabash in a canoe, he, with his brother, settled on the almost unbroken prairies of Illinois. Adopting the law as a profession, he was deemed an equal at least of Douglas and Lincoln. In 1845, he was elected to Congress. When war was declared with Mexico, he raised a regiment and was under General Taylor. When General Shields fell at Cerro Gordo, the gallant Baker became the commander of his brigade.

At the close of hostilities, Colonel Baker removed to California. In October, 1859, when Senator Broderick was killed by Judge Terry, "because he was opposed to slavery and a corrupt administration," Baker was a fitting orator to pronounce his eulogy. Both of them, the living and the dead, were self-made men; and the son of the stone-cutter, lying in mute grandeur, with a record floating round that coffin that bowed the head of the surrounding thousands down in mute respect, might have been proud of the tribute which the weaver's apprentice was about to lay upon his breast. For minutes after the vast audience had settled itself to hear his words, the orator did not speak. He did not look in the coffin—nay, neither to the right nor left; but the gaze of his fixed eye was turned within his mind, and the still tears coursed rapidly down his cheek. Then, when the silence was the most intense, his tremulous voice rose like a wail, and with an uninterrupted stream of lofty, burning and pathetic words, he so penetrated and possessed the hearts of the sorrowing multitude, that there was not one cheek less moistened than his own. For an hour he held them as with a spell; and when he finished, by bending over the calm face of the noble corse, and stretching his arms forward with an impressive gesture, exclaimed, in quivering accents, "Good friend! brave heart! gallant leader! hail and farewell!" the audience broke forth in a general response of sobs. Never, perhaps, was eloquence more thrilling; never, certainly, was it better adapted to the temper of its listeners. The merit of the eulogy divided public encomiums with the virtues of the deceased, and the orator became invested with the dead Senator's political fortunes. He soon after removed to Oregon, where, in 1860, he was elected Senator for six years. Nor was he long in making his mark in that renowned assembly. His replies to the sophistry of Benjamin, on the question of secession, combining argument and eloquence, logic and wit, placed him in the very front rank of senatorial orators. The words he then spoke thrilled through the country, and prepared the way for that grand uprising of the nation a few weeks later.

At the outbreak of this most wicked rebellion, Baker was one of the first to rush to the field. At the great meeting of the people in Union Square, on the 19th of April, 1861, he was among the most earnest of the speakers. He was, however, not only a speaker; he was a doer as well; and soon he had gathered about him as effective a regiment as ever engaged in a campaign. His regiment soon became a brigade, and the government would have made him a major-general, had he not wished to retain his seat in the United States Senate. He was at first stationed at Fortress Monroe, whence he was transferred to the upper Potomac, under the command of Brigadier-General Charles P. Stone.

On the morning of the 21st of October, Colonel Baker received orders to cross the river with his brigade, and make a reconnoissance toward Dranesville. The place of crossing selected by General Stone was Ball's Bluff—a steep, clayey bank, fourteen feet high—the transportation, two old scows, holding about thirty-five men each, propelled by poles across the deep and rapid stream. Surmounting all obstacles, the stream was crossed, the bank ascended, and the brave leader found himself in a thick forest, surrounded by the enemy. Sustained by the gallant Bramhall's two guns, he held the rebels at bay for hours; but his men were falling like grass before the scythe. Having been reinforced, he placed himself at the head of his regiment and heroically charged on the overwhelming ranks of the enemy, but he became the mark for a dozen rifles, and the noble leader and orator, matchless of the earth, fell mute, to speak no more!

"As in life, no other voice so rang its trumpet blast upon the ear of freemen, so in death its echoes will reverberate amid our mountains and our valleys, until truth and valor cease to appeal to the human heart.

'His love of truth—too warm, too strong
For Hope or Fear to chain or chill—
His hate of tyranny and wrong,
Burn in the breasts he kindled, still.'

Good friend! brave heart! gallant leader! hail and farewell!"

MAJOR-GENERAL IRVIN McDOWELL, U.S.V.

> "Tell me who thou art;
> What generous source owns that heroic blood,
> Which holds its course thus bravely?"

IRVIN McDOWELL was born in Franklin county, Ohio, on the 15th of October, 1818. He was sent, at the age of fourteen years, to a military academy in France, where he acquired a knowledge of the French language, and the first principles of military discipline. Returning to the United States in 1834, he entered the Military Academy at West Point, and graduated in 1839. Appointed to a second-lieutenancy in the first artillery, he was immediately ordered to Lake Ontario, and subsequently to Holton, Maine, where he continued until all danger of a war between the United States and England was averted. Lieutenant McDowell was then ordered to West Point, and in October, 1842, was promoted to a first-lieutenancy, and remained at the Academy in the position of adjutant until October, 1845, when he was selected by General Wool as aide-de-camp, and accompanied that general through the Mexican War. For gallant services in the battle of Buena Vista, on the 23d of February, 1847, he was breveted captain, and in May following appointed assistant adjutant-general.

At the close of the Mexican War he was transferred to the staff of General Scott; with the exception of the time he was in Texas, on a tour of inspection, and of one year which he passed in Europe, he continued with the commander-in-chief till the outbreak of the rebellion, of 1861, at which time he held the rank of major and assistant adjutant-general, which had been conferred upon him on the 31st of March, 1856. Had his advice, urged by the commander-in-chief upon the President, been followed, nearly the whole army, of some twelve thousand regulars, would have been concentrated in Washington by the 4th of March, 1861, and the Government been enabled immediately to have crushed the rebellion. But Mr. Buchanan feared to avail himself of his military resources, and nearly one-half of the regular army was forever lost to us; and soon rebel bands occupied Alexandria, the heights of Arlington, the southern extremity of the long bridge, and threatened destruction to the city.

Major McDowell, then acting under the authority of General Scott, displayed great activity and energy in preserving the city from the rebels. He even organized the builders and the stone-cutters of the Capitol into companies, opened a well in the cellar, and established a bakery there; and if the city had been captured, he was prepared to hold that building as a citadel until the Northern troops should come to its rescue. Other public buildings were also fortified and garrisoned by the District militia. Fortunately, the sixth and eighth Massachusetts and seventh New York brought timely aid and secured the safety of Washington.

On the 14th of May following, Major McDowell was appointed a brigadier-general of volunteers, and placed in command of the right bank of the Potomac. The appointment of major-general in the regular army was also offered him and declined.

His management during the advance of the army to Bull Run, the temporary success of our troops, the sudden panic and disastrous route, are well known.

On the accession of General McClellan to the chief command, General McDowell received the command of a division in the army of the Potomac, which he retained until promoted to that of the first corps of the army of the Potomac. On the 14th of March, 1862, he was appointed a major-general of volunteers. His next command was that of the Department of the Rappahannock, which was created on the 4th of April, 1862, and included that part of Virginia between the Potomac and the Acquia, Fredericksburg and Richmond Railroad on the east, the Blue Ridge on the west, and so much of Maryland as is between the Patuxent and the Potomac, and also the District of Columbia and the city of Washington.

This command he exercised under the orders of the President and War Department, and his acts and movements were in accordance therewith. It was retained until suppressed, together with the Mountain Department and the Department of the Shenandoah, and the whole placed under the command of General Pope.

The part which General McDowell acted, in the retreat of General Pope before the overwhelming forces of the enemy—a retreat slow, difficult, and ably conducted, till the army had arrived within helping distance of the forces near Washington—won the warm approval of General Pope, and expressions of admiration from officers who knew his devoted and energetic services during the great perils to which that army had been subjected. On arriving at Washington, General McDowell little expected to find himself the object of popular indignation and abuse. With a clear conscience, on the 6th of September, he requested the President to relieve him of the command of the third corps, and grant a court of inquiry into his whole conduct. The President acceded to the request, and the court was composed of Generals Cadwalader, Martindale, and Van Allen.

General McDowell married, in 1849, Miss Helen Burden, the daughter of Henry Burden, of Troy.

Always dignified, frequently frigid and silent in his manner, he will at times give full play to the fine impulses of his nature, and surprises the listener by the warmth and kindness of his heart, the vigor and clearness of his ideas, the breadth and beauty of his conversation, and the fascinating power of his address. While keenly sensitive to the feelings and good-will of his soldiers, he never resorts to the flattery of words or manner to gain their applause, but is quietly assiduous in promoting their personal comfort and welfare as far as consistent with the success of a campaign and the public good.

MAJOR-GENERAL A. E. BURNSIDE, U.S.V.

> "The nerves of fiery Manhood, in many a danger tried,
> With the quick blood of young Valor, to the calm of years allied,
> With the hero's eagle glances, and the sage's thoughtful face,
> Mark the Leader called by Providence to Peril's lofty place."

AMBROSE EVERETT BURNSIDE was born at Liberty, Union county, Indiana, on the 23d of May, 1824. In 1842, he entered the West Point Military Academy, and graduated in 1847, with the rank of brevet second-lieutenant in the Second United States Artillery. In September of the same year he was promoted to a full second-lieutenancy and transferred to the Third Artillery, and was attached to Captain Bragg's company, with which he marched in the division of General Patterson to the city of Mexico. In the Indian border wars of New Mexico he distinguished himself in an encounter with the Apache tribe in August, 1849, near Los Vegas. For his gallantry on this occasion he was, in December, 1851, promoted to the rank of first-lieutenant. Subsequent to this he was stationed at Fort Adams, in Newport Harbor, and retired from service in October, 1853.

He went to Chicago, April 27th, 1858, and obtained a situation as cashier in the Land Department of the Illinois Central Railroad. In June, 1860, he was elected treasurer of the company and removed to New York, where he resided at the breaking out of the great rebellion of 1861.

When the First Regiment of Rhode Island Volunteers was raised, Governor Sprague tendered Mr. Burnside the command, which he immediately accepted, and on the 24th of April, 1861, he arrived in Washington with twelve hundred men, ready for any emergency.

Upon the advance toward Manassas, in July, Colonel Burnside was placed in command of a brigade in Colonel Hunter's division. They left Washington on the 16th, and on the 21st was fought the disastrous battle of Bull Run. In the flank movement, Burnside's brigade took the advance, and soon after crossing Bull Run, they were attacked by the enemy. Colonel Hunter was wounded very early in the action; and Colonel Burnside, being in command, led his brigade forward, and succeeded in beating back the enemy and driving him from that part of the field. At length, having stood the brunt of the battle for two hours, it was withdrawn to replenish its exhausted supply of ammunition. The order then coming to fall back, Colonel Burnside's retreat was conducted in good order, and the brigade entered Washington about nine o'clock on the morning of the 22d of July.

The term of service of the three months' volunteers having expired, Colonel Burnside and his regiment were mustered out of the service and received the thanks of the General Assembly of Rhode Island. His services were also recognized by the nation at large, and on the 6th of August, 1861, he was made a brigadier-general of volunteers, and was summoned to Washington, where he greatly assisted in reorganizing the forces in front of the capital.

Early in January, 1862, a noble armada left Annapolis, freighted with munitions of war and fifteen thousand men, commanded by the indefatigable Burnside. While nearing Cape Hatteras, a most terrific storm burst upon them, and continued for a week with such force as seemed to indicate the entire destruction of the fleet. Thanks to the almost superhuman efforts of their noble commanders, the calamity was averted and their destination reached in safety.

Harassed by the delays caused by the storm, active operations could not be immediately commenced. On the 5th of February, however, the whole fleet steamed slowly up toward the entrance of the Sound. On the 6th, the gunboats entered Croaton Sound, defeated the rebel fleet and bombarded their batteries on Roanoke Island. On the afternoon of the 7th, the troops were landed; and on the morning of the 8th, the attack was made upon the key of the position, a strong battery in the centre of the island. The battle lasted two hours and resulted in a most complete victory of the national forces, who covered themselves with glory. Congress gave him thanks for the great success, and the President nominated him a major-general of volunteers. The Senate confirmed the nomination on the 18th of March, 1862.

Meanwhile, General Burnside was not idle. On the 7th of March the capture of Newbern was decided after a desperate struggle of four hours, by a brilliant bayonet charge, the rebels fleeing precipitately, burning the bridges after them, and rendering pursuit impossible. Soon after, Fort Macon was invested and reduced. Reno and Hawkins were sent northward, where they fought the bloody battle of Camden. Indefatigable still, Burnside opened communication with Norfolk and Fortress Monroe by the Dismal Swamp Canal. Hearing in July of the disastrous battles before Richmond, he hastened to McClellan's aid, but too late to save him. The Peninsula was lost, and even Burnside's skill could not restore it.

General Burnside is one of the truly great men of this age and nation. There is no blemish in his character, no stain on his fair escutcheon. Prudent without timidity, brave without rashness, religious without pretence, and wholly engaged in the great cause which has enlisted his powers, General Burnside nobly unites the best qualities of a soldier and a man.

MAJOR-GENERAL D. C. BUELL, U.S.V.

"Brave Gael, my pass, in danger tried,
Hangs in my belt, and by my side."

DON CARLOS BUELL was born on the banks of the Muskingum River, in the State of Ohio, on the 23d of March, 1818. He entered the West Point Military Academy in 1837, and, graduating there in 1841, was appointed a brevet second-lieutenant in the Third Regiment of United States Infantry. He was promoted to a first-lieutenancy in June, 1846, accompanied his regiment to Mexico, and on September 23d was breveted captain for gallant and meritorious conduct at Monterey. His regiment joining General Scott's army at Vera Cruz, he distinguished himself at Contreras and Churubusco; was severely wounded in the latter action, and was breveted major. In January, 1848, he became assistant adjutant-general with the rank of captain; relinquished his rank in the line in March, 1851, and was employed in the duties of his office in various parts of the country.

After the commencement of hostilities in 1861, he materially assisted in the organization of the army at Washington. In August he was appointed a brigadier-general of the volunteer service of the United States, dating from May 17th, 1861, and assigned to a division in the army of the Potomac, which soon became distinguished for its thorough discipline. In November he superseded General W. T. Sherman in command of the Department of the Ohio, with headquarters at Louisville, Kentucky. On the 17th of December a portion of his forces gained a victory at Mumfordsville; and in February, 1862, after the capture of Fort Henry, his advance under General Mitchel marched upon the Confederate stronghold of Bowling Green, which was hastily evacuated.

On the 21st of March, 1862, the President promoted General Buell to the rank of major-general of volunteers, and on the same day his department was incorporated with that of the Mississippi under General Halleck. On the night of the 6th of April he arrived with a part of one division at Pittsburg Landing just in time to succor Grant's wearied force. Three of his divisions coming up on the following day, the rebels were driven behind their intrenchments at Corinth. By order of General Halleck, dated June 12th, he took command of the new district of Ohio, comprising the States of Kentucky and Tennessee, east of the Tennessee River, and so much of northern Alabama and Georgia as might be held by the national troops. He also occupied and fortified posts extending east and west from Iuka, Mississippi, to Bridgeport, Alabama, about one hundred and fifty miles—a line which had previously

MAJOR-GENERAL D. C. BUELL, U.S.V.

been secured by General Mitchel—and north and south from Nashville, Tennessee, to Decatur, Alabama, nearly the same distance, with his headquarters at Stevenson or at Huntsville, Alabama.

Chattanooga was held by a strong force of rebels under Braxton Bragg, who threw from thence large bodies into East Tennessee, the occupation of which had been supposed to be the ultimate object of General Buell. Meantime the rebels captured Murfreesborough on the 12th of July, taking prisoner General T. T. Crittenden and other officers stationed there. On the 22d they attacked Florence, Alabama, capturing a Federal detachment and destroying an immense quantity of army stores and other property, which operations they continued with equal success at several other points. Gallatin was taken, together with General Johnson and seven hundred men, on the 21st of August; and on the 29th they severely defeated Generals Manson and Nelson near Richmond, Kentucky, compelling the abandonment of Lexington and Frankfort, and the removal of the State archives to Louisville.

The advance of Bragg, under Kirby Smith, had before this time penetrated into Kentucky, and threatened Louisville and Cincinnati; and Bragg himself, masking his movements, had marched northward with his main force. Tennessee and Kentucky were also overrun with rebel guerillas, who inflicted terrible cruelties and suffering upon the Unionists. General Buell commenced evacuating his posts on the 23d of August to follow Bragg on a shorter line of march. On the 14th of September his main army occupied Bowling Green, while Bragg's was encamped at Glasgow, thirty miles east. On the same day, Buckner attacked Mumfordsville, and the attack being renewed with augmented force on the 16th, the place was captured with over four thousand prisoners. It was reoccupied on the 24th by General Buell, who, at midnight of the same day, entered Louisville, which had been for some time occupied by General Nelson.

On the 1st of October, by order of the President, General Buell turned over his command to General Thomas; but on the same day, at the urgent request of the latter, he was restored, and immediately commenced the pursuit of the rebels, then somewhat scattered, but chiefly encamped at Bardstown, while most of their generals were engaged at Frankfort in inaugurating a provisional Confederate State government. The rebels having retreated to Perryville, a severe but indecisive battle was fought with them there on the 8th by a portion of Buell's army. On the 18th, Lexington, which had been reoccupied, was again captured by a thousand rebel cavalry, but immediately abandoned. On the 23d, General Bragg, by slow marches, had reached Cumberland Gap, lately evacuated by the Federal general, Morgan, who had held it for many months, and General Buell had ceased his pursuit.

On the 24th of October, 1862, General Buell was ordered to transfer his command to General Rosecrans, and to report himself at Indianapolis, which he did on the 30th; and subsequently a court of inquiry, to investigate his operations in Kentucky, was ordered to meet at Cincinnati on the 27th of November.

MAJOR-GENERAL JOHN POPE, U.S.V.

"His sword the brave man draws,
And asks no omen but his country's cause."

JOHN POPE was born in Kentucky in the year 1822. He was appointed a cadet in the West Point Military Academy from Illinois in 1838, graduated in 1842, and on the 1st of July he received his commission as brevet second-lieutenant of topographical engineers. In the Mexican War he was attached to the army of General Taylor. For "gallant and meritorious conduct" at Monterey, he was breveted a first-lieutenant on the 23d of September, 1846, and for his gallantry in the battle of Buena Vista he received the brevet of captain, February 23d, 1847.

In 1849 he conducted the Minnesota exploring expedition, and acted as a topographical engineer in New Mexico until 1853. From 1854 to 1859 he was engaged in the exploration of the Rocky Mountains. On the 1st of July, 1858, he took the rank of captain in the corps of topographical engineers.

In February, 1861, Captain Pope was one of the officers appointed by the War Department to escort President Lincoln to Washington. On the 17th of May, 1861, Captain Pope was appointed a brigadier-general in the volunteer service of the United States, and his appointment was confirmed by the Senate on the 3d of August. He was very active in northern Missouri, in reopening and protecting railroad communication and driving out guerillas.

When General Halleck was appointed to the command of the department, he placed General Pope at the head of the Army of the Mississippi, destined to coöperate with Flag-Officer Foote's flotilla. This was in December, 1861. On the 17th of that month he scattered the rebel camp at Shawnee Mound, and on the 18th he surprised another camp near Milford. This campaign drove Price below the Osage River. He was next appointed to clear Southeastern Missouri. On the 23d of February, 1862, he reached Commerce with a small force. He there gathered his men together, and in six days marched through the swamps to the rear of New Madrid with twelve thousand men. He immediately laid siege to it and cut off its supplies.

On the 15th of March, Commodore Foote invested the rebel stronghold at Island No. 10. Pope, at New Madrid, cut off all communication by the river from below thus completing the investment. Through the almost superhuman efforts of Colonel Ellet, a canal, thirteen miles in length, was dug across the point, through which a gunboat and transports were sent him from above. This enabled him to cross the river and take the batteries on the other shore; and everything was in readiness for an assault when, at midnight on the 7th of April, two rebel officers boarded our boats to surrender the island. Thus, after a vigorous siege of twenty-one days, the "Gibraltar" of the enemy fell into our hands.

On the arrival of General Halleck at Pittsburg, after the battle of Shiloh, General Pope was ordered to join him, which he did in five days, and was placed on the extreme left of the army besieging Corinth. He soon became convinced that Beauregard was evacuating that position, and begged permission in vain from Halleck to attack the divided rebel force. In vain he chafed against the restraints of his superior, who lay supinely within five miles of the enemy, while the wily rebel stole away. He, however, was allowed the privilege of pursuing the retreating rebels, but with little effect. While engaged in this pursuit, General Pope was called to Washington by the President's special order of June 26th, to take command of the Army of Virginia. About this time General Pope was made a brigadier-general of the regular army, *vice* General Wool, promoted.

He commenced active operations on the 19th of July, and, by his great activity, compelled the rebels to send out a large force to check his advance, thus enabling McClellan to escape from the Peninsula. On the 29th, he took the field in person. On the 2d of August the Rapidan was crossed, and Orange Court House taken possession of. Then came the famous battle of Cedar Mountain, fought by General Banks on the 9th of August. Though Jackson had greatly the advantage, yet Banks, after a hot artillery duel, charged his batteries, and held his own against terrible odds until nightfall, when he withdrew out of range. On the morning of the 10th, Sigel took the front, and met every plot with a counterplot. Jackson, finding himself outmanœuvred, retreated on the night of the 11th, pursued by Milroy and Buford, and outflanking Pope, who was checking Lee in front. Hearing of Jackson's movement, Pope evacuated Warrenton and retreated to the old battle-field of Bull Run.

The second battle of Bull Run was commenced on the 27th of August by the defeat of Ewell by Hooker. On Thursday, the 28th, McDowell and Sigel came up with Jackson, and a terrific conflict ensued that lasted till darkness separated the combatants. In the night, Jackson's reinforcements came up, and on the next day, the 29th, the fighting was terrible. Each party fought with the desperation of fury. To the rebels, defeat would strike a death-blow to their confederacy; to the federalists, it would be a disgrace which few cared to contemplate. By night, Jackson was driven back to Gainesville, and the next morning the battle was resumed. Jackson was forced over Catharpin Creek, but Pope was too wearied to pursue.

On the 6th of September he preferred charges of insubordination against Generals McClellan, Porter, Franklin, and Griffin, and demanded a court of inquiry; but, at the request of McClellan, the President stayed the proceedings, and General Pope was given the command of the Department of the Northwest. The Sioux had risen and committed massacres in that department, and a bloody Indian war hovered over our frontier.

MAJOR-GENERAL S. R. CURTIS, U.S.V.

"Qui sunt qui penetrant hostis penetralia? Giraldidæ.
Qui sunt qui patriam conservant? Giraldidæ.
Qui sunt quos hostes formidant? Giraldidæ.
Qui sunt quos livor detractet? Giraldidæ."

SAMUEL R. CURTIS was born in Licking county, Ohio, on the third of February, 1807, of Connecticut parents. Entering the West Point Military Academy at the age of twenty, he graduated in 1831, receiving on the 1st of July the commission of brevet second-lieutenant in the seventh regiment of infantry, but resigned on the 30th of June, 1832. He studied and pursued the profession of law in Ohio, and was subsequently an engineer in Ohio and Iowa. From April, 1837, to May, 1839, he served as civil engineer on the National Road, and especially as chief engineer on the Muskingum improvement. In 1842 he returned to the law, and became a successful practitioner in Wooster, Ohio, and afterwards in Iowa.

On the breaking out of the war with Mexico he was elected colonel of a volunteer battalion, which position he resigned on receiving the appointment of adjutant-general of Ohio, for the special purpose of mustering volunteers. From June 23d, 1846, to June 24th, 1847, he served as colonel of the Third Ohio Volunteers. He was civil and military governor of Matamoras, Comargo, and Monterey, and commanded the twelve hundred men who pursued Urrea from Comargo to Remas, opening the way to General Taylor after the battle of Buena Vista. After the discharge of his regiment he served on the staff of General Wool, and as governor of Saltillo.

After the war he removed to Iowa, practised law, and was appointed chief-engineer of the Des Moines River improvement. From 1850 to 1853 he was engineer in charge of the harbor and other works of the city of Saint Louis, and during the two following years chief engineer of the American Central Railroads. In 1856 he was elected to Congress, and in 1858 reëlected, serving both terms on the Pacific Railroad and Military Committees. He was also a member of the Peace Convention, and in 1860 was again reëlected to Congress.

When the reverberation of Sumter's guns reached his ears, he left his Western home, and joining the Seventh New York at Philadelphia, he marched with them to Washington as aide to Colonel Lefferts. On the 1st of June, 1861, he was commissioned colonel of the Second Iowa Volunteers, with which regiment he left Keokuk on the 12th for Northern Missouri, where he rendered good service in ridding it of guerillas. On the 23d of June he went to Washington to attend the extra session of Congress, and on his return, took command of Jefferson Barracks, having been made a brigadier-general of volunteers, to date from the 17th of May, 1861.

On the 12th of September he was given the command of the Benton Barracks, where he rendered important services in drilling and organizing the troops. From November 9th to December 25th he commanded the Saint Louis District of the Department of Missouri. On the 26th of January, 1862, he left Rolla in command of an expedition into Arkansas. The army was composed of three divisions, commanded by General Sigel, and Colonels Davis and Carr. Frequent skirmishing was continued along the line of march from Springfield until the total defeat of Price in the great three days' battle in the Cross Hollows, known as the battle of Pea Ridge.

The army remained near the battle-ground nearly a month, expeditions being frequently sent out to disperse guerilla bands which were forming along the border. On the 21st of March, 1862, General Curtis was promoted to the rank of major-general of volunteers, for gallant and meritorious conduct in his Southwestern campaign; and early in April he was ordered to move eastward to Batesville, on the White River, where the army remained several weeks, during which time an expedition was sent out to Searcy, in White county, in the direction of Little Rock.

General Curtis at length left Batesville, on the 23d of June, determined to make his way to the Mississippi River. The enemy continually obstructed the roads, and skirmishes took place almost daily. Near Cotton Plant and Round Hill a considerable battle was fought, in which the rebels were defeated and driven beyond the White River. From Clarendon to Helena, on the Mississippi, the march was one of the most fatiguing character, and the army suffered greatly from the excessive heat and dust, and scarcity of provisions and water.

On arriving at Helena, General Curtis established his headquarters in the fine residence of the rebel general Hindman, and sent out expeditions into the country to disperse guerilla bands, and down the Mississippi to capture or destroy flatboats loaded with supplies for the rebel army. The steamer "Fair Play," laden with arms and munitions of war, was captured; and a force was sent up the Yazoo River, where a field battery was captured, and several heavy guns destroyed.

On the 28th of August, 1862, General Curtis received a leave of absence from the War Department to attend the Pacific Railroad Convention; and on the 19th of September he was assigned to the command of the Department of the Missouri. Five days afterwards he assumed command of the department, and established his headquarters at Saint Louis.

MAJOR-GENERAL FRANZ SIGEL, U.S.V.

> "I do not think a Braver Gentleman,
> More active-valient, or more valient-young,
> More daring, or more bold, is now alive,
> To grace this latter age with noble deeds."

FRANZ SIGEL was born at Zinsheim, in the Grand Duchy of Baden, November 18th, 1824. He received a liberal education, and graduated from the military school at Carlsruhe, whence he entered the regular army of Baden. On the breaking out of the great rebellion of 1848, Lieutenant Sigel threw up his commission and joined the Liberals, and was placed second in command of the revolutionary army, and was made minister of war by the "Provisional Government." He was present and greatly distinguished himself at the battles of Grossacken, Waghausel and Ettlingen, and on the flight of Mieroslawski, assumed command of the army, and made a masterly retreat to Rastadt. But the members of the Provisional Government were already fugitives; Rastadt was invested, and Sigel was compelled to fly to Switzerland; but, driven from there by the decree of the Helvetic Confederation, he came to the United States in 1850.

On his arrival, he became a teacher in Dr. Dulon's academy, and, marrying his daughter, took up his residence in New York. He also became the major of the Fifth Regiment, New York State Militia, Colonel Schwarswaelder. In September, 1858, Major Sigel removed to St. Louis, and was employed in teaching until the breaking out of the rebellion.

Known as a soldier of experience, he obtained a colonel's commission and organized a regiment of his countrymen, which, under the designation of the Third Missouri, was incorporated May 15th, 1861, in General Lyon's First Missouri Brigade. Colonel Sigel participated in the capture of Camp Jackson, and afterwards did good service in intercepting rebel supplies. He left St. Louis on the night of June 11th, for the southwestern part of the State. Arriving at Sarcoxie with only his own regiment, he was informed that Price was encamped at Neosho with nine hundred men; and the next morning, June 29th, he marched to attack him, but he broke up his camp and fled. Sigel was joined at Neosho by Colonel Salomons, and he pushed on to attack the rebels, whom he met about nine miles above Carthage. After a bloody battle of two hours, Sigel's ammunition gave out, and he was obliged to retreat to his baggage train, where he made a stand and defeated the enemy.

In the battle of Wilson's Creek, on the 10th of August, Colonel Sigel commanded the second column, which attacked the rebel's right and drove them half a mile from their position, but his advance was broken by the fire of a regiment that he permitted to approach, believing it to be a reinforcement from General Lyon, and he was driven back. He retreated to Springfield, where he assumed the command on learning the death of General Lyon, and the next morning retreated to Rolla before the overwhelming force of the enemy.

Colonel Sigel was appointed a brigadier-general of volunteers on the 17th of May, 1861, but did not receive his commission till the 17th of August. On the 19th, he arrived at St. Louis, where he remained several weeks conferring with General Fremont. He arrived at Sedalia and took command of Fremont's advance there, September 28th, and on October 13th, marched from that place for Warsaw; crossed the Osage on the 16th, and arrived at Springfield with his commander October 27th. When General Fremont was removed from the command on the 2d of November, Franz Sigel headed the signatures to a paper expressing great regret and dissatisfaction at the course of the government in removing their beloved general. The next day General Hunter arrived and took command; a retreat to St. Louis was ordered, and southern Missouri again became a prey to rebel invasion. General Sigel was left inactive, and "while his name rang, like that of Mars, from every German lip throughout the Union," he was unnoticed and neglected, and, on being superseded by General Curtis, December 27th, he felt that gross injustice had been done him, and four days later, sent in his resignation. No notice being taken of it, he tendered it a second, and finally, a third time, when the government declined to accept it.

On the 11th of February, 1862, General Curtis left Lebanon, and with Sigel in the advance, he pursued the flying enemy into Arkansas; but, finding the rebels in overwhelming numbers at Bentonville, he fell back to Pea Ridge, thus leaving Sigel in his rear with only one thousand men. In this responsible position, the gallant German found four thousand of the enemy, half cavalry, attempting to cut off his baggage train; but he was too active for them, having sent it off under a guard of two hundred men. The rebels attacked him and were repulsed; they surrounded him and he cut his way through; they enveloped him and attacked him on all sides at once, and he beat them off with the most heroic valor. Through the long day he fought, and at night succeeded in joining the main body. The next day, March 7th, the enemy renewed the battle in full force, and by nightfall they were again repulsed. At daybreak the next morning, Sigel charged with the left wing and drove the rebels from the heights; soon after, a general charge was made, which completely routed the enemy, driving him in confusion through the impassable defiles of Cross Timber.

But his great exertions proved too much for him, and he was obliged to return to St. Louis, where he remained for some time. Meanwhile, he had been made a major-general, and on his recovery, was assigned a command in the Army of Virginia.

His name will be immortal in the country he has served so well.

MAJOR-GENERAL J. A. McCLERNAND, U.S.V.

> "*Strike*—till the last armed foe expires;
> STRIKE—for your *altars* and your fires;
> STRIKE—for the green graves of your sires;
> GOD—and your native land!"

JOHN ALEXANDER MCCLERNAND was born in Breckinridge county, Kentucky, on the 30th of May, 1812. Upon the death of his father, four years later, his mother moved to Shawneetown, Illinois, where John alternately attended school and worked on a farm. After studying law for three years, he was admitted to the bar in 1832. In the same year he volunteered in the war against the Sacs and Foxes, serving in the ranks until the war terminated in the battle of Bad-axe. On his return, his ill health unfitting him for professional pursuits, he traded, in 1833–'34, upon the Ohio and Mississippi Rivers. In 1835 he established the "Shawneetown Democrat," and resumed the practice of law.

In 1836, 1840, and 1842, Mr. McClernand was elected to the State legislature, and in 1843 a representative in Congress. His first speech there was in favor of the bill to remit the fine imposed upon General Jackson by Judge Hall. During the second session of the same Congress he introduced a bill for a grant of land to aid in the completion of the Illinois and Michigan Canal. In 1844 he was reëlected without opposition, and again in 1846 and 1848. He was chairman of the Committee on Resolutions in the Democratic State Convention of 1858, which sustained the course of Senator Douglas on the Lecompton bill. In 1860 he was elected to Congress for the Springfield district, and served until the breaking out of the rebellion.

He then returned home, and, with Colonels Logan and Finke, raised the McClernand brigade. The President appointed him a brigadier-general of volunteers on the 17th of May, 1861, and assigned him to the Cairo district, whence he accompanied General Grant to Belmont, where he did good service. In his field order No. 145, dated Fort Donelson, February 18, 1862, General McClernand says:

"Being the first division to enter Fort Henry, you also pursued the enemy for miles, capturing from him in his flight six field pieces, many of his standards and flags, a number of prisoners, and a great quantity of military stores.

"Following the enemy to this place, you were the first to encounter him outside of his intrenchments, and drive him within them.

MAJOR-GENERAL J. A. McCLERNAND, U. S. V.

"Pursuing your advantage, the next day you advanced upon his lines, in the face of his works and batteries, and, for the time, silenced them.

"The next day you daringly charged upon his redoubts, under a deadly fire of grape and canister, and were only prevented from taking them by natural obstacles, and the accumulated masses which were hurried forward to defend them.

"The next day you extended your right, in the face of newly-erected batteries, quite to the Cumberland, thus investing his works of nearly two miles.

"The next day, after standing under arms for two days and nights, amid driving storms of snow and rain, and pinched by hunger, the enemy advanced in force to open the way to his escape. By his own confession, formed in a column of ten successive regiments, he concentrated his attack upon a single point. You repulsed him repeatedly, often driving back his formidable odds. Thus, after three days' fighting, when your ammunition was exhausted, you fell back until it came up, and re-formed a second line in his face. Supported by fresh troops, under the lead of a brave and able officer, the enemy was again driven back, and, by a combined advance from all sides, was finally defeated. His unconditional surrender the next day consummated the victory.

"The battle-field testifies to your valor and constancy. Even the enemy accorded to you an unsurpassed heroism, and an enviable and brilliant share in the hardest fought battle and most decisive victory ever fought and won on the American continent." McClernand and his division were covered with glory!

For gallant and meritorious conduct in the siege and battles of Fort Donelson the President rewarded General McClernand by appointing him a major-general of the volunteer forces of the United States, March 21st, 1862.

At the bloody battle of Shiloh, on the 6th of April, he fought with undaunted heroism throughout that eventful day. The battle of the next day was fought with even more bravery and gallantry, McClernand alternately winning and losing four times the ground in front of his division. We all know the result. Beauregard was driven into his intrenchments, Halleck took command of the Federal army, and the traitor stole away unharmed. General McClernand served with the army of Tennessee, under Major-General Grant, until the autumn of 1862, when he was ordered to the command of the army of the Mississippi.

MAJOR-GENERAL LEWIS WALLACE, U.S.V.

"What man dare, I dare."

GENERAL WALLACE is a native of Indiana, born at Brookville, Franklin county, A.D. 1827, and is a son of Ex-Governor Wallace, long a leading citizen of the State. In personal appearance, General Wallace is rather above medium height, of a symmetrical, muscular development, straight as an Indian, dark complexioned, with a keen, piercing black eye; in bearing, he is the perfect soldier, of commanding presence, yet genial deportment; in popularity, he is, to use the words of a correspondent of his division, "idolized by the men under his command." From boyhood, military science and soldier life have been General Wallace's beau ideals; and, although, perhaps, the youngest general of his rank in the army, he is as old, in all that makes generalship, as many who have grown grey in the service. Nor did the great rebellion find him altogether inexperienced in actual service on the field, having served as a lieutenant in the Mexican War.

After the Mexican War closed, he entered the profession of the law, and finally located in Crawfordsville, where he resided at the commencement of the rebellion. Yet, while engaged in the practice of the law, the general never forgot the soldier-dreams of his youth. On July 4th, 1856, he organized the Montgomery Guards, and in 1859, he introduced the peculiar drill, including the bayonet exercises, of the French Zouaves; and so earnestly did they strive to acquaint themselves with the intricacies of that most difficult drill, that, in the fall of 1860, General Wallace had, by common consent, the best drilled company west of the mountains. Of its members, thirty are now holding, or have held, commissions in our volunteer army, ranging in rank from major-general to lieutenant.

Much has been said of Indiana's soldiers, so well have they sustained themselves on every field, and with such terrible emphasis have they given the lie to the vile calumniation of Jeff. Davis, uttered against them on the plains of Mexico, that they have given to their State a reputation second to none in the Union. Of the glorious name and rank thus achieved, none can more justly be proud than General Wallace; for it is largely the workmanship of his own hands.

The day following the fall of Sumter, General Wallace, then attending court in a neighboring county, was called to Indianapolis, by Governor Morton, and appointed Adjutant-General. On receiving the call, he did not even go home for a day's preparation; but, leaving everything, obeyed, instantly, the call of his country, then only just awakening from what had almost proved her death slumber. In an incredibly short time, General Wallace set the war machinery of the State in motion; and, from a quiet agricultural district, the State became, in a single week, a vast military camp. He organized the six regiments first called out, and himself accepted a colonelcy of the famous Eleventh. His regiment, being the first ready for the field, was ordered to Evansville, to keep in check the threatened uprising in Kentucky. When that danger was passed—when Kentucky's sons remembered the heroic deeds of their sires, and, shaking off the incubus of neutrality which had well nigh crushed them, had again seized the sword, to vindicate once more their name and honor, under the old flag, he was ordered to Cumberland, Maryland.

While stationed at the latter place, General Wallace, with a portion of his regiment, made a forced march of eighty-eight miles (forty miles by rail and forty-eight by foot) to Romney, Va., dispersing a body of rebels collected at that place, accomplishing the entire object of the expedition in twenty-nine hours. For this feat he was handsomely complimented by General Scott, then commander-in-chief. From Cumberland, General Wallace was ordered to Harper's Ferry, where he remained until after the battle of Bull Run.

The term of enlistment of the regiment having expired, it returned to Indianapolis, and was mustered out. A majority of its members reënlisted, and the whole regiment was quickly recruited for the three years' service. Wallace and his regiment were ordered to St. Louis, and thence to Paducah. On the 3d of September, General Wallace received his commission as Brigadier-General, and immediately had a brigade assigned him, of which his old regiment, the Eleventh, and the no less famous Eighth Missouri regiment, were a part. At the battle of Fort Donelson, General Wallace commanded the division that regained, by unrivalled valor and superior tactics, the ground lost by McClernard's Illinois regiments, and stormed one side of the enemies' works; while the gallant General Smith (now no more) won imperishable honor by his heroic charge upon the opposite side of the fort.

On the 18th of February, 1862, General Wallace was nominated by the President as Major-General, for gallant conduct at Fort Donelson, and was unanimously confirmed by the Senate. From Donelson, General Wallace was ordered to Pittsburg Landing, Tenn.; and, at the commencement of the great battle, was stationed, with his division, at Crump's Landing, some ten miles below the battle-field. He arrived with his division on the field of Shiloh, Sunday night, and spent the night in arranging his men and laying his plans for the battle, which morning light would certainly bring upon him. On Monday morning he waited not for an attack, but himself opened the fight, which turned defeat into glorious victory. It is enough to say that General Wallace on that day commanded a division which did hard fighting, and which gave back before the enemy "NEVER AN INCH."

MAJOR-GENERAL W. S. ROSECRANS, U.S.V.

> "Onward, my hero! Men shall catch the flame,
> Which lights thy soul, and glow again for shame.
> With thee, and such as thee, we shall reclaim
> The morning glory of our empire's fame!"

WILLIAM STARKE ROSECRANS was born in Kingston, Delaware county, Ohio, on the 6th of December, 1819, where he passed his early life, a hard student. On his own direct application to Honorable Joel R. Poinsett, Secretary of War, he was appointed a cadet in the United States Military Academy at West Point, whence he graduated with honors in 1842; received the brevet of second-lieutenant of engineers on the 1st of July, and was ordered to Fortress Monroe, where he served as first assistant engineer to Lieutenant-Colonel De Russey. In August, 1843, he married Miss Ann Eliza Hegeman of New York, and in September was ordered to West Point to act as assistant professor of engineering and natural philosophy. After remaining four years at West Point he was transferred to Newport, Rhode Island, and made engineer-in-chief of the fortifications at Fort Adams during his stay there, from 1847 to 1853. From April, 1853, he was constructing engineer at the Washington Navy Yard. He tendered his resignation in November, 1853, and again in April, 1854, when it was accepted, and he retired from the service.

He commenced in Cincinnati as a civil engineer and architect. In 1855 he accepted the superintendency of the Cannel Coal Company of Coal River, Kanawha Court House, Virginia, and the presidency of the Coal River Navigation Company, which he retained until April, 1857, when he returned to Cincinnati, and engaged in the manufacture of kerosene oil.

When McClellan was made a major-general of Ohio volunteers he appointed Rosecrans acting chief engineer, with the rank of major, and the Legislature soon made him chief engineer of that State with the rank of colonel. On the 10th of June, Governor Dennison appointed him colonel of the Twenty-third Regiment of Ohio Volunteers; and, on the 20th of June, 1861, the President appointed him a brigadier-general of the regular army of the United States.

General Rosecrans participated in the earliest advance into Western Virginia; and, on the 11th of July, defeated General Garnett in the battle of Rich Mountain. Cutting his way through a thick growth of mountain pines and heavy under-brush for nearly nine miles, he came upon the rebels on the hill-top, and, after a hard fight of an hour, completely routed them, and then pushed on to Beverly. The fruit of this prompt action was the surrender of Colonel Pegram and his whole force.

MAJOR-GENERAL W. S. ROSECRANS, U. S. V.

On the 22d of July, General McClellan was ordered to Washington, and General Rosecrans assumed command of the Department of the Ohio. Leaving Clarksburg on the 31st of August, he reached the rebel intrenchments at Carnifex Ferry on the 10th of September, and, after a slight skirmish, routed Floyd, and captured all his arms, stores, etc.

By the President's War Order No. 3, dated March 11th, 1862, the Mountain Department was created, and General Fremont ordered to command it. General Rosecrans accordingly bade farewell to his troops at Wheeling on the 29th, and repaired to Washington. The special order of the President, June 26th, 1862, ordered General Pope to the command of the army of Virginia, and General Rosecrans took his place at the head of the army of the Mississippi. In recognition of his valuable services, and for gallant and meritorious conduct, the President promoted him to the rank of major-general of volunteers in the following July.

Price, emboldened by Buell's inactivity, invaded Tennessee with fifteen thousand men, and occupied Iuka about the 17th of September. Rosecrans left Rienzi, and on the afternoon of Friday, the 19th, surrounded Price's superior numbers and attacked him on three sides. Price, however, made a desperate charge and cut his way out with great loss. At daybreak the battle was resumed. Cavalry, infantry, and artillery were entangled in horrible confusion, and the carnage was dreadful. About noon, the enemy's lines became disordered; he wavered, and finally fell back. Our forces made a magnificent charge, and the rebels were swept like chaff before the storm. Routed at all points, they fled in disorder; Rosecrans following in hot pursuit, capturing many prisoners and a large army train.

Price, though terribly defeated, was not disheartened; and, after a junction with Van Dorn and Lovell, returned. This time Rosecrans was encamped at Corinth, Mississippi, where Price attacked him on the 3d of October. Price pushed on victoriously, driving our forces within their intrenchments. In attempting to repulse him, General Hackelman fell bravely fighting at the head of his brigade. On the morning of the 4th, Price made an attack on our left, and after a most deadly contest, drove in our centre, and penetrated to the heart of the town, where they were stopped, and soon fled in disorder, pursued by General Hamilton. Meanwhile, Van Dorn led a most determined charge on our extreme right, through the abbattis. Two of their columns reached the ditch, and the other stopped within fifty paces of it. All that grape and canister would do was tried; but when the rebels reached the point, a charge was ordered, when it became a race between the twenty-seventh Ohio and the seventeenth Missouri, which proved too much for the staggered rebel columns. Terrified, they broke and fled in wild confusion, leaving their dead and wounded on the field of battle. Rosecrans was again victorious! And again he was deservedly rewarded. On the removal of General Buell, the President appointed General Rosecrans to the command of the department.

MAJOR-GENERAL O. M. MITCHEL, U.S.V.

> "Mitchel! strong brain, quick eye, and steady hand!
> Faithful in service—faultless in command;
> Thou favorite son of science!—fit to stand
> Foremost among the saviours of the land!"

ORMSBY MCKNIGHT MITCHEL was a native of Kentucky, having been born there, in Union county, on the 28th of August, 1810. He was appointed a cadet in the West Point Military Academy in 1825, and on graduating, July 1st, 1829, received the commission of second-lieutenant in the second regiment of artillery. August 30th, 1829, he was appointed acting assistant professor of mathematics at West Point, which position he retained until the 28th of August, 1831. He resigned his military rank on the 30th of September, 1832; began the study of law, and practised in Cincinnati for two years. From 1834 to 1844 he held the position of professor of mathematics, philosophy, and astronomy in the Cincinnati College, in Ohio. From 1836 to 1837 he was chief engineer of the Little Miami Railroad, and in 1841 was one of the Board of Visitors to the West Point Military Academy. He became the founder and director of the Cincinnati Observatory in 1845, and retained the latter position for several years, during which time he edited and published the "Sidereal Messenger." In 1847 he was appointed adjutant-general of Ohio, and in 1848 chief engineer of the Ohio and Mississippi Railroad. In 1858, when the troubles in the Dudley Observatory left it without a manager, Professor Mitchel was called to the vacant post. Such is the brief history of the gallant general before his entrance on the stage of the great slaveholders' rebellion of 1861.

At the great meeting at Union Square, New York, Professor Mitchel was one of the principal speakers, and his oration was unequalled for patriotic fervor and splendid imagery. His devotion to the Union was not unheeded; for on the 9th of August, 1861, the President appointed him a brigadier-general in the volunteer force of the United States from New York. He was ordered to the Department of the Ohio, where he engineered that series of fortifications around Cincinnati that checked the audacious march of Kirby Smith upon that city.

His command rapidly increased from a brigade to a division, and then a column. He took Cynthiana, and then, in rapid succession, seized every other point on the railroads reaching to Lexington and Frankfort, and controlling the entire north and centre of the State.

On the 15th of February, 1862, he occupied Bowling Green, after a forced march of forty miles over almost impassable roads, in twenty-eight hours. Astonished at his appearance, Buckner fled precipitately, leaving the "Gibraltar of Kentucky," with its immense accumulation of military stores, to fall into the hands of the Federal troops.

After the occupation of Nashville he moved down the railroad leading from that city to Chattanooga, where he was doubtless expected; but suddenly, and without any previous notice of his movements, we find his force to have turned on to a branch line to Fayetteville, and, by a grand forced march across the country, he turns up in possession of a point of their main southern trunk line of railroad, the rebel's principal route of communication, midway between their two principal points of occupation at Chattanooga and Corinth. Here he seized a quantity of rolling stock, and by its aid he secured one hundred miles of the railroad. Having removed from Huntsville to Florence and Decatur, destroying as he went the railroad bridges and connections, in order to prevent pursuit and cut off all reinforcements from the rebels, we next find the bold and dashing astronomer-soldier at Iuka, Mississippi, in the rear of Beauregard's left flank, and but twenty miles distant from him.

After the evacuation of Corinth he greatly assisted in the operations in the West. He defeated the rebels at Winchester, and drove them back to Chattanooga, thus preventing a movement. At the latter place he totally defeated and routed the rebel force after two days' severe fighting. He did not go unrewarded, for on the 15th of April, 1862, the President recognized his valuable services by appointing him a major-general in the volunteer service of the United States.

In September, General Mitchel was withdrawn from the field of his successes; why it is needless now to ask. After many weeks of weary waiting, he was given, on the 8th of October, the command of the Department of the South, with headquarters at Beaufort. He left with a weight upon his heart. It was the shadow, no doubt, of his coming death. He felt that this assignment South was, in some sense, a putting him aside where he could be of no use; nevertheless, he obeyed his Government, and went to Beaufort. He had small means of work at hand, but he only redoubled his energies to make the most of what he had. He at once set himself about the business of reorganizing the forces, and by the exercise of his usual industry and perseverance had about completed the preparations for the projected new campaign, when he was taken sick with yellow fever, and, after a brief illness, died on the 30th of October, 1862.

Doubtless he overtasked his fiery spirit. Struggling against fearful odds, and burning within with impatient zeal, and burnt without by the fervid heats of an unaccustomed clime, his gaze grew dim that never blinked before in gazing among the stars, and the film of death settled forever upon his earthly vision. The eye that had perused the heavens in rapt glory, measuring the mightiness of God in his systems of worlds, found its last joy in greeting the stars of his country's flag, beneath which and for which his earnest and great life was ebbing away.

MAJOR-GENERAL C. M. CLAY, U.S.V.

"March at the head of the ideas of your age, and then these ideas will follow and support you. If you march behind them, they will drag you on; and if you march against them, they will certainly prove your downfall."

CASSIUS MARCELLUS CLAY, one of "Nature's noblemen," who has ever marched at the head of the ideas of his age, was born in Madison county, Kentucky, on the 19th of October, 1810. After studying for some time in the Transylvania University at Lexington, in his native State, he entered Yale College, and, graduating in 1832, returned to Kentucky, where he commenced the study of law. In 1835 he was elected to the State legislature. In the following year he was defeated, but was triumphantly reëlected in 1837. In 1839 he was a delegate to the Harrisburg Whig Convention, which nominated General Harrison for the presidency.

Removing to Lexington, he was elected to the legislature from Fayette county in 1840. The improved jury system, and the common school system of Kentucky, are, in a great measure due to the energetic efforts of Mr. Clay. He denounced the Texas annexation scheme as designed for the extension of slavery; and in 1844 traversed the Northern States, addressing immense audiences in favor of the Whig presidential candidate.

On the 3d of June, 1845, he issued, in Lexington, Kentucky, the first number of the "True American," a weekly newspaper, devoted to the overthrow of slavery in that State. It aroused indignant opposition; and while he was sick, in the following August, his press was seized by a mob and sent to Cincinnati. He was threatened, by public resolution, with assassination; but, continuing steadfast in his noble course, upon recovering, he revived his paper, printing it in Cincinnati, and publishing it in Lexington. Public sentiment came gradually to support the principles of freedom of the press, and Mr. Clay was able to keep an anti-slavery journal in the field, first at Lexington, and afterwards at Louisville.

Upon the declaration of war against Mexico, in 1846, he entered the service as captain of the Old Infantry, a volunteer company which had already distinguished itself in the battle of Tippecanoe, in 1811, and which was now converted into dragoons. He reached Monterey while it was the headquarters of General Taylor, and was detached from his regiment and ordered to the van of the army at Saltillo. Under command of Major Gaines, who was ordered to advance and find the enemy, Captain Clay was taken prisoner January 23d, 1847, at Encarnacion, over one hundred miles in advance of the main army, and, with seventy-one associates, was marched through San Luis Potosi, to the city of Mexico. On one occasion, when a portion of the party escaped, the gallant bearing and presence of mind of Captain Clay saved the remainder from massacre. He was exchanged, and on his return home was presented, in the autumn of 1847, by his fellow-citizens, with a sword in honor of his services.

In 1848 he labored vigorously for the nomination of General Taylor for the presidency by the Whig National Convention, in opposition to the friends of Henry Clay. In 1850 he separated from the Whig party, and presented himself as a candidate for governor of Kentucky, on the basis of a political organization against slavery. He canvassed the whole State amid great excitement and peril, and received nearly five thousand votes, thus defeating the Whig nominee for the first time in more than twenty years.

In the famous presidential campaign of 1856 Mr. Clay labored earnestly and untiringly for the election of Mr. Fremont, identifying himself with the interests of the Republican party. In the campaign of 1860 the anti-slavery cause again received his hearty support, and he contributed not a little to the election of Mr. Lincoln. About the time of the inauguration of the newly-elected President, an attack upon Washington by the rebels, aided by the traitors in the capital, was confidently expected; and early in March, 1861, Cassius M. Clay hastily formed an organization of visitors and citizens for the protection of the city. This organization was known as the "Clay Guard," and many distinguished statesmen, civilians, and soldiers served in its ranks.

On the 28th of March, Mr. Clay received the appointment of minister plenipotentiary and envoy extraordinary to the court of St. Petersburg. He accompanied to England Mr. Adams, minister to the court of St. James, and soon after his arrival in London wrote, May 17th, to the London "Times," an able, keen, and eloquent letter, which, exposed its author to many attacks and criticisms from the press of that country.

He was cordially and honorably received at the Russian court by Prince Gortschakoff, who heartily sympathized with the cause of the United States, and earnestly wished for the consummation of that holy cause of universal emancipation, so nobly, so heroically inaugurated by his brave young Czar. But Mr. Clay could not bear to be away from his country in the hour of her peril. He wished to strike a blow himself in her defence, and after nearly a year's residence at St. Petersburg he was recalled, at his earnest request, and his place filled by Mr. Cameron.

On the 11th of May, 1862, the President appointed Cassius M. Clay a major-general in the volunteer service of the United States, and while awaiting orders to use his sword in his country's cause, he used his tongue, in fervid eloquence, in her behalf.

MAJOR-GENERAL J. L. RENO, U.S.V.

"Ω Ξειν' αγγειλον Λακεδαιμονιοις, οτι τηδε
Κειμεθα, τοις κεινων πειθομενοι νομιμοις."

JESSE L. RENO was born in Virginia in the year 1825. His family removed to Pennsylvania when he was a boy, and from that State he was appointed to West Point in 1842. He graduated in 1846, ranking seventh in a class which included "Stonewall" Jackson, McClellan, and others, and was appointed brevet second-lieutenant of ordnance on the 1st of July. He immediately went to Vera Cruz, where he took command of his howitzer battery, which he led through every battle from Vera Cruz to Mexico. For gallant and meritorious conduct at the battle of Cerro Gordo he was breveted first-lieutenant, his commission bearing date April 18th, 1847. For bravery on the battle-field of Chapultepec, where he was wounded, he was breveted captain September 13th, 1847. When hostilities ceased he was appointed assistant professor of mathematics at West Point for six months, and was then appointed secretary of the Board of Artillery—a position he held about eighteen months, during which he was engaged in testing the relative merits of heavy ordnance and compiling a work on heavy artillery tactics. He was subsequently connected with the Coast Survey service; and upon withdrawing, went out West with a corps of topographical engineers, and assisted in the construction of a military road from Big Sioux to Saint Paul. He was engaged in this work some twelve months, and on the 3d of March, 1853, he was promoted to a full first-lieutenancy of ordnance. He was next stationed at the Frankfort Arsenal, in 1854, where he remained about three years, and then accompanied General Johnston in the expedition to Utah, as ordnance officer. Returning in 1859, he was ordered to the Mount Vernon Arsenal in Alabama, and was subsequently stationed at Fort Leavenworth, Kansas. On the 1st of July, 1860, he was promoted to a captaincy of ordnance, having been senior first-lieutenant of that department for some time.

Captain Reno was appointed a brigadier-general of volunteers November 12th, 1861, and was subsequently ordered to report to General Burnside at Annapolis, Maryland, preparatory to taking a command in the expedition to North Carolina, which sailed from Fortress Monroe on the 12th of January, 1862, and arrived at Cape Hatteras a few days later.

On the 6th and 7th of February, Roanoke Island was bombarded by our gunboats. On the afternoon of the 7th, General Burnside landed his troops; and on the morning of the 8th, an attack was made upon the key of the position, a strong battery in the centre of the island. While General Foster, at the head of the central column, attacked the battery in front. General Reno, at the head of the left column, attempted to attack the enemy's right flank. After a severe march of two hours through a densely wooded swamp, which the rebels supposed to be inaccessible, he debouched from the woods on their right as Hawkins' Zouaves charged on their front. Surprised, they fled precipitately, and Reno hoisted the stars and stripes on the abandoned battery. Colonel Shaw soon after surrendered, and the victory was complete.

Reno's blood-stained laurels were next to be gathered at Newbern's hard-won batteries. Landing below the city on the afternoon of March 13th, they bivouacked all night in the dreary rain. The next morning Parke and Foster took up the line of march on the left, while Reno followed up the railroad on the right. Moving steadily up, he bravely attacked the enemy's redans near the railroad. For a long time a heavy fire was kept up, and the carnage was terrible, when Reno, Parke and Foster simultaneously charged on the batteries and carried them at the point of the bayonet. Newbern was ours, and Burnside made it his headquarters.

In April he was sent to Camden, North Carolina, where he carried the enemy's batteries with heavy loss, and compelled the enemy to retire to Norfolk.

In July, General Reno's division was ordered to Newport News to reinforce the Army of the Potomac, and from thence to Fredericksburg. He was soon attached to the Army of Virginia, and showed his usual gallantry in the second great battle of Bull Run, which terminated on the 1st of September. In this battle he supported McDowell and Heintzelman, many times repulsing the enemy, and so distinguishing himself that his name is among the foremost of those honorably mentioned in the reports.

When General McDowell received his leave of absence, General Reno was appointed to the command of his corps d'armée, and a few days later he received the commission of a major-general of volunteers "for gallant and meritorious conduct" in the late great battles. He sought the advance again in the march on the rebels in Maryland, and, alas! we now have to mourn his loss.

On the 14th of September the rebels were attacked at South Mountain. General Reno had been most active all day, and death seemed to shun his ubiquitous person. About seven o'clock the fight was over, the victory was won; and just as he was congratulating his staff upon the happy termination of the day, a Minie ball struck him in the breast. He fell from his horse and was instantly borne to the rear, where, beneath a fine old Maryland tree, under which lovers had whispered, children played, and old women drowsed, the soul of a brave man passed off to the Illimitable. Thus died one of the bravest generals that was in the service of his country—one of the bright gems in the crown of Burnside, and a man whom all respected and loved. A younger man than Kearney, he bade fair to become as splendid a soldier as that lamented general; and in his death the army and the country have lost one whom we could not well spare. He lived long enough to win for himself an honorable fame in our history.

MAJOR-GENERAL E. O. C. ORD, U.S.V.

> "You wrong yourself, brave sir; your martial deeds
> Have ranked you with the great."

EDWARD OTHO CRESAP ORD was born in Maryland in the year 1818. His father served as an officer both in the army and navy during the war with Great Britain in 1812-15. His mother was a Cresap, of the famous border family of that name, to one of whom—though, as since proved, unjustly—the Indian Chief Logan has in his last speech attached such a cruel celebrity. Edward entered the United States Military Academy in 1835 and graduated in 1839, in the same class with General Halleck. Assigned as second-lieutenant to the third regiment of artillery, he at once joined his regiment in Florida, and during the next three years was actively engaged and much distinguished in the war then waging against the Seminole Indians. In Harney's expedition into the Everglades, he generally led the advance, and on one occasion, after wading for four miles through water and grass—the water from two to four feet deep—he, with a party of seven men, attacked some eight or ten Indians who were lying concealed upon a little island, and four of his men being almost immediately wounded, the rest fled, and he was left alone, with one badly wounded man, whom he would not desert, until the arrival of reinforcements compelled the Indians to make their escape in boats.

From 1842, when his regiment was ordered out of Florida, until 1845, when he was detailed on the Coast Survey, he was employed on garrison duty, part of the time with Ringgold's celebrated battery at Fort McHenry, Maryland, but chiefly at Fort Macon, North Carolina. In June, 1846, just after the opening battles of the Mexican War, he sailed for California with his company on board the United States ship "Lexington," accompanied by Lieutenants (now major-generals) Halleck, of the engineers, and William T. Sherman, of the third artillery. He remained on duty in California throughout the war and until 1850, part of the time in command of the little city of Monterey, and part of the time engaged in making maps of the country, or in expeditions after Indians, horse-thieves and murderers. In 1848 he was sent by General Mason, with two soldiers, in pursuit of four or five desperate murderers, who had fled from the mines. After following them down the country for three hundred miles unsuccessfully, crossing the San Luis Mountains twice, while separated from his party, in a snow storm and alone, he finally succeeded in having them arrested, by sending on a native, who, riding forty leagues, induced the people of Santa Barbara to turn out, pursue and capture them. He then had them tried—himself acting as prosecutor—before a jury of six Americans and six Californians, and the evidence of their guilt being clear, had them all shot.

In 1850, Lieutenant Ord was sent East by General Riley, with dispatches, but returned to California the same year, and remained there on topographical duty, until some time in 1851, when, being promoted to a company then stationed in Boston harbor, he joined it, and served with it nearly two years. In 1853 he was again ordered on the Coast Survey, and continued on that duty, part of the time along the coast of Florida and Georgia, part of the time along the coast and coast islands of California, until May 19, 1855, when he joined his company, now serving in California.

During Captain Ord's stay in California in 1854, he was married to a pretty and amiable daughter of Judge R. A. Thompson, of that State, by whom he has five children. From 1855, with the exception of two years spent as instructor at the artillery school at Fort Monroe, Virginia, he remained uninterruptedly on duty with his company in California, Oregon and Washington Territory, and took an active and prominent part in the Indian wars upon that coast, especially the Rogue River war of 1855 and 1856, and the brilliant campaign against the confederated tribes of Washington Territory in 1858. The first decided victory ever gained by our troops over the warlike tribes of Rogue River in Oregon, was achieved by Captain Ord; it broke their courage, and soon led to their complete submission.

Appointed brigadier-general of volunteers, September 14, 1861, he immediately started for the East, and was, on his arrival, assigned to a brigade in the division composed of the Pennsylvania reserve corps, commanded by General McCall, and soon after fought and won the battle of Drainsville, in Virginia. This victory, gained as it was over the flower of the rebel army, commanded by their celebrated cavalry general, Stuart, in person, did much to restore the *morale* of our troops, somewhat shaken by previous reverses. For this achievement, General Ord was promoted to the rank of major-general of volunteers, his commission bearing date May 2d, 1862, and was ordered to report for duty, as such, with the army of the Mississippi, under Major-General Halleck, who placed him in command of the town of Corinth and of two divisions of his army.

On the 5th of October, at the battle on the Hatchie, General Ord gallantly drove the enemy, taking two batteries, and over two hundred prisoners. Just before the fight was over, he was severely wounded by a minie-ball passing through his ankle between the bones, cutting the Achilles' tendon and fracturing both bones slightly.

To talents of a very high order, General Ord adds qualities of the heart, which have made him deservedly popular among his men. At one time, jumping overboard and saving, at the risk of his own, the life of a drowning soldier; at another, sucking the wound inflicted by a rattlesnake's deadly fangs upon a brother-officer; he has always been found ready to risk his life for others.

MAJOR-GENERAL JOSEPH HOOKER, U.S.V.

> "It is held
> That valor is the chiefest virtue, and
> Most dignifies the haver: if it be,
> The man I speak of cannot in the world
> Be singly counterpois'd."

JOSEPH HOOKER was born in Hadley, Hampshire county, Massachusetts, in the year 1815. He entered the West Point Military Academy in 1833, and on graduating with honors in 1837, received the commission of second-lieutenant in the first artillery. In February, 1838, he was appointed assistant commissary of subsistence, and promoted to a first-lieutenancy. From July to October, 1841, he acted as adjutant at the Military Academy; and from 1841 to 1845, he ranked as regimental adjutant. When the war with Mexico broke out, he was appointed aide-de-camp to General Hamer, and greatly distinguished himself throughout the war. He was breveted captain in 1846 "for gallant conduct in the several conflicts at Monterey on the 21st, 22d and 23d of September, 1846." In March, 1847, he was appointed assistant adjutant-general, with the full rank of captain; and, in the same year, was breveted major "for gallant and meritorious conduct in the affair at the National Bridge, on the 11th day of June, 1847." "For gallant and meritorious conduct in the battle of Chapultepec," September 13th, 1847, he was breveted lieutenant-colonel. This ended his valuable services in the Mexican War. In 1848 he rose, in regular line of promotion in his regiment, to a full captaincy; and in the same year vacated his regimental commission and accepted the appointment of assistant adjutant-general, with rank of captain, which position he continued to fill until 1853, when he resigned while on duty in California, purchased a tract of land, and became a farmer in Sonoma, on the Bay of San Francisco. From this employment, when the Government made an appropriation for a national road connecting California and Oregon, he was summoned to superintend that enterprise by Colonel Bache, who was in charge of that appropriation, and who well understood his capacity and fidelity. General Hooker had just finished this work and returned to California, when, like Cincinnatus, he was literally summoned from his plough to fight the battles of his country.

At the first reverberation of the artillery of Fort Sumter upon the shores of the Pacific, he started immediately for the field of conflict, and on his arrival there was appointed by the President a brigadier-general in the volunteer service of the United States, on the 17th of May, 1861. His appointment was confirmed by the Senate on the 3d of August. General Hooker was immediately placed in command of a brigade in the army of the Potomac, consisting of the first and eleventh Massachusetts, second New Hampshire and twenty-sixth Pennsylvania regiments of volunteers. This brigade soon obtained the well-earned *sobriquet* of "Hooker's Fighting Brigade." He was subsequently put in command of a division; and from July, 1861, to the following February, he was in Southern Maryland, on the north shore of the Potomac. While there, he chafed to cross over with his men, drive the enemy back, and relieve Washington from its blockade. But this was not permitted.

General Hooker accompanied McClellan to the Peninsula, and took a prominent part in the whole campaign, and gained fresh laurels in every engagement. The battle of Williamsburg, on the 5th of May, was one of the most stubborn and hard-fought battles of the war. With but eight thousand men, General Hooker held in check the combined divisions of Longstreet and A. P. Hill, numbering twenty thousand men, from early morning until four or five o'clock in the afternoon, when Kearney came so gallantly to his assistance, and drove the enemy through Williamsburg.

At Fair Oaks, he was placed in front of the enemy on the Williamsburg stage road, and repeatedly drove back their reconnoitering forces, not once being driven from any position he took. Again he displayed his valor, and a fresh laurel was added to his already crowded wreath. In the various minor contests, Hooker took his part and bravely went through with his share of the seven days' fights. At Nelson's Farm and at Malvern Hill, his fighting division never faltered, but stood their ground nobly, and repulsed the enemy whenever they attempted to advance. For "gallant and meritorious conduct" in this disastrous campaign, General Hooker was promoted to the rank of major-general in the volunteer service of the United States. It was a just, though tardy recognition of his great services.

The pretended advance of General Pope on Richmond, released McClellan from his beleaguered position at Harrison's Landing; and on the 22d of August, 1862, the Peninsula was evacuated. Heintzelman's corps d'armée joined Pope on the old battle-field of Bull Run; and we find the names of "Fighting Joe Hooker" and Kearney mentioned as being together in the thickest of the struggle.

Then came South Mountain and Antietam, where he was again the Marshal Ney of the fight. For nearly the whole day, he fought the entire rebel army single handed, meeting the shock without flinching, and driving them back full a mile, when he was shot in the foot by a rebel rifle ball, and compelled to retire from the field. Had he not been wounded when he was, the rebel army would have been entirely annihilated.

For his gallant conduct in these battles, he was made a brigadier-general in the regular army of the United States, to fill the vacancy occasioned by the fall of Mansfield. It was a just and well-earned tribute. He has, in the most emphatic as well as triumphant manner, literally fought his way to his present elevation; and no man better deserves the title of "**The Bravest of the Brave**."

MAJOR-GENERAL S. P. HEINTZELMAN, U.S.V.

"The tyrant custom, most grave senators,
Hath made the flinty and steel couch of war
My thrice driven bed of down."

SAMUEL P. HEINTZELMAN was born at Manheim, Lancaster county, Pennsylvania, in 1805; graduated at West Point in 1826; breveted second-lieutenant of third infantry in 1826; second-lieutenant of second infantry 1827; first-lieutenant in 1833; captain in 1846. Was appointed captain in the Quartermaster's Department United States army during the Creek War in Alabama. In 1846, when the law passed separating the staff from the line of the army, he resigned his staff commission and went into Mexico as captain of the second infantry, and was breveted major for gallant conduct at the battle of Huamantala, Mexico. In 1848 he was ordered to California, and assigned the command of the Southern District. In 1850, the Indians became troublesome, but the wholesome severity he used, brought the tribes into subjection, so that the Indians of Southern California have ever since been peaceable; for which service he was breveted by the President lieutenant-colonel.

Ordered to Yuma in 1851, he remained until 1854; was promoted to major in 1855. From 1855 to 1857 he was stationed at Newport Barracks, Kentucky; joined his regiment in 1858, in Texas, as major of the first infantry. When the Cortinas difficulty broke out, he was ordered by General Twiggs from Camp Verdé to take command of the forces on the Rio Grande. After several engagements with the Mexicans, he dispersed Cortinas' band, and drove them back into Mexico.

Foreseeing the political difficulties of the country, he obtained leave of absence, and reported at Washington in February, 1861. He was stationed at Governor's Island in April. In May he was ordered to Washington as acting inspector general. On the 21st of May he commanded the first troop that crossed the Potomac into Virginia, and at midnight took possession of Arlington Heights and the surrounding country. May 14th he was made colonel of the Seventeenth United States Infantry, and ordered to command the troops at Alexandria.

At the battle of Bull Run he commanded the extreme right of the army, and was wounded in the arm, late in the day of the 21st of July, when leading up the Brooklyn Fourteenth against the enemy, which wound was aggravated by being fourteen hours in the saddle, after receiving it, commanding our rear guard.

He was made brigadier-general of volunteers, and in October, was ordered to the command of a division on the left of the army of the Potomac.

MAJOR-GENERAL S. P. HEINTZELMAN, U. S. V.

On the 8th day of March, 1862, the army of the Potomac was reorganized and formed into five corps d'armée, General Heintzelman being assigned to the command of the third corps, and ordered to the Peninsula. General Heintzelman's troops were the first to land there, and in the advance of the army in its march on Yorktown; and on the evacuation of Yorktown, they were ordered in pursuit of the enemy.

On the 5th of May, General Heintzelman fought the battle of Williamsburg. Here his two divisions (Hooker's and Kearney's) not only covered themselves with glory, but established now, for the first time, the fighting reputation of the army of the Potomac.

The army advanced on Richmond, and, after crossing the Chickahominy, Heintzelman was placed in command of the left wing, consisting of the third and fifth corps.

On the 1st of June, at the battle of Fair Oaks, General Heintzelman repulsed the enemy, and drove them back toward their defences at Richmond. During this battle the general's horse was shot under him. The right wing of the army having received a severe check at the battle of Gaines' Mills, was ordered to make a flank movement toward the James River. During this march (known as the week of battles), the troops commanded by General Heintzelman were invariably successful in repelling the heavy columns of the enemy attacking our army on the flank and rear.

On the arrival of the army at Harrison's Landing, he was promoted to the rank of major-general. During the retreat eventually ordered from Harrison's Landing, he was detached to a most exposed point to cover the flank of the army.

Embarking at Yorktown on the 20th of August, General Heintzelman was ordered, with his corps, to report to General Pope, to aid in protecting the railroad to the Rappahannock. On the 26th, his troops were all ready in position. The enemy having turned the right of the army under General Pope, and having cut our line of communication, Heintzelman was ordered, with Hooker's division, to reopen the line. The enemy was found in force at Kettle Run, and was brilliantly and successfully repulsed. The army now followed in pursuit of the Confederates, and found them, on the 29th, strongly posted on the plains of Manassas. Being in command of the right wing, Heintzelman immediately engaged the enemy, and succeeded toward night in driving them from their original position. The next day he maintained his line, refusing reinforcements until the centre and left of our army gave way, when he was directed to fall back on Centreville. On the retreat, a portion of his first division (Kearney's) repulsed the enemy successfully at Chantilly.

Heintzelman was soon after placed in command of all the troops and forts south of the Potomac; and since the departure of General Banks he has been in command of all the troops and forts composing the defences of Washington.

MAJOR-GENERAL SILAS CASEY, U. S. V.

> " A breath of submission we breathe not ;
> The sword that we've drawn we will sheath not !
> Its scabbard is left where our martyrs are laid,
> And the vengeance of ages has whetted its blade !"

SILAS CASEY, the hero of Fair Oaks, was born in the town of East Greenwich, Rhode Island, on the 12th of July, 1807. In 1822 he was appointed from Rhode Island to the Military Academy at West Point, where, in 1826, he graduated as brevet second-lieutenant of the seventh infantry. Lieutenant Casey was first stationed at Fort Towson, on the Red River, in the Indian Territory. With the Indians of that country he had several skirmishes. In 1829 he was stationed at Sackett's Harbor, on Lake Ontario.

On the 12th of July, 1830, he was married to Miss Abbie P., daughter of the Honorable Dutee I. Pearce, who was fourteen years delegate to the House of Representatives from Rhode Island.

Lieutenant Casey was subsequently stationed at Fort Niagara, Lake Ontario, and at Fort Gratiot, Michigan, in 1833. In 1835, during the Creek War, he was stationed at Tuskegia, Alabama. In 1836 he was promoted to a first-lieutenancy, and in the capacity of assistant quartermaster and commissary, with the rank of captain, was attached to a regiment of Creek Indians which marched against the Seminoles. In 1839 he was commissioned as captain, and for gallant conduct at the battle of Pilaklikaha was recommended for a brevet majority. He was afterwards stationed at Buffalo and Fort Mackinaw.

During the Mexican War, in 1847, he was with the command of General Scott. On the day before the storming of Contreras, Captain Casey and his command repelled the attack of a body of Mexican lancers, and killed their leader, General Fronterd. At Contreras he commanded the leading division of one of the columns of attack, where his company received the enemy's first fire, and afterwards assisted in capturing one hundred and fifty Mexican lancers. On the same day, Captain Casey was one of the first who entered the fort at Churubusco, where he planted the colors of the second infantry, and for his gallant conduct received the brevet of major. At Chapultepec, Major Casey, in command of a storming party, was severely wounded. For his bravery on this occasion he received the brevet of lieutenant-colonel.

In 1849, Colonel Casey established the post of Benicia, near San Francisco.

In 1854 he was made a member of a board which assembled at Washington and West Point to revise infantry tactics. In 1855 he was commissioned lieutenant-colonel of the ninth infantry, of which he organized six companies, and was subsequently placed in command of the department of Puget Sound, where he finished an Indian war in thirty days, reducing to submission five hundred Indians. During the San Juan question with Great Britain, the island was occupied and fortified by Colonel Casey, who was ready for a vigorous defence if required by our Government.

On the 31st of August, 1861, he was appointed a brigadier-general of volunteers, and assigned a division in the corps of General Keyes, with whom he went to the Peninsula in the following March. On the 9th of October, 1861, he was promoted to the colonelcy of the fourth regiment of infantry.

In the disastrous Peninsular campaign his part was comparatively an unimportant one, save in the bloody and memorable battle of Fair Oaks, where, on the 31st of May, 1862, Johnston and Longstreet, with forty thousand men, taking advantage of a terrible storm which had flooded the valley of the Chickahominy, attacked his worn-out division of but five thousand. Bravely the little band again and again repulsed the enemy's serried ranks, fighting for five hours, until one-third of them lay dead on the gory field. Their noble commander had two horses shot under him, and performed many a valorous deed on the hard-fought field. In the afternoon, Keyes arrived at the scene of conflict, closely followed by Heintzelman and Sumner, and at night the wearied armies slept on the battle-field. In the morning the enemy renewed the conflict, but were everywhere repulsed, and fled at nightfall.

General McClellan, who arrived upon the field after the battle was over, after a dispatch which he was afterwards obliged to retract, further injured the brave commander and his gallant, suffering division, by superseding the former by General Peck, and sending him back to the White House. This command General Casey retained until the withdrawal of McClellan from the Peninsula, when, after successfully evacuating the White House, he repaired to Washington, of whose defences he was at once ordered to assume command. He was also assigned to the command of the Provisional Brigades; and in November, 1862, was appointed one of the court-martial for the trial of General F. J. Porter. On the 26th of May, 1863, the board for the examination of officers of colored troops was organized, and General Casey was appointed its president. He has ever since continued in the admirable performance of the arduous and important duties of these positions, with almost incalculable benefit to the service and the nation.

General Casey is an able tactician, disciplinarian, and mathematician. The suns of Mexico and the snows of Oregon may have silvered the locks and bent the frame of the general, but they have neither sapped his energy, dimmed his intellect, nor chilled his heart. On others circumstances have conferred a more wide-spread fame and more dazzling reputation, but the Muse of History can inscribe on her page the name of no servant to his country more single-hearted than Silas Casey.

MAJOR-GENERAL FITZ JOHN PORTER, U.S.V.

> "For love-lorn swain, in lady's bower,
> Ne'er panted for the appointed hour,
> As I, until before me stand
> This rebel chieftain and his band."

FITZ JOHN PORTER was born in New Hampshire about the year 1824, and at the age of seventeen entered the West Point Military Academy, where he graduated in 1845, receiving a second-lieutenancy in the Fourth Regiment of United States Artillery on the 1st of July. In May, 1847, he was promoted to the rank of first-lieutenant, and accompanied General Scott to Mexico. For gallant and meritorious conduct at Molino del Rey, he was breveted captain. At Chapultepec he again distinguished himself, and obtained the brevet of major. At the fight at the Belen Gate of the city of Mexico, he was severely wounded. On the return of the army to the United States, he was appointed Assistant-Instructor of Artillery at West Point, which office he filled until the outbreak of the rebellion.

On the increase of the army on the 14th of May, 1861, Fitz John Porter was appointed colonel of the new fifteenth infantry, and, three days afterwards, brigadier-general of volunteers. A command was given him in the army of the Potomac. He rendered useful aid to General McClellan in reorganizing the army after the battle of Bull Run, and was soon placed in command of a division. He accompanied the army to Yorktown, and was there placed in command of the siege-works. After the evacuation of the place, he was for a while governor of Yorktown, but soon resumed his place in the advancing army. On the 25th of June he commanded the extreme right of our army, and bore the brunt of the terrible battles of the 26th and 27th.

For gallant and meritorious conduct in the Peninsula campaign, General Porter was promoted to the rank of major-general of volunteers, his commission bearing date July 4th, 1862.

MAJOR-GENERAL W. B. FRANKLIN, U.S.V.

> "Is it the thunder's solemn sound
> That mutters deep and dread,
> Or echoes from the groaning ground
> The warriors' measured tread?
> Is it the lightning's quivering glance
> That on the thicket streams,
> Or do they flash on spear and lance
> The sun's retiring beams?"

WILLIAM BUELL FRANKLIN was born in York, Pennsylvania, February 27th, 1823. Entering the West Point Military Academy in 1839, he graduated in 1843, at the head of his class, in which were Major-Generals Grant, Reynolds, and Augur. On the 1st of July he was commissioned a brevet second-lieutenant in the corps of topographical engineers, stationed on the survey of the Northern lakes. In the summer of 1845 he accompanied General Kearney's expedition to the south pass of the Rocky Mountains, and in the following year was engaged in the survey of Ossabaw Sound, Georgia.

Reporting to General Wool at San Antonio, Texas, in August, 1846, he accompanied him to Saltillo, Mexico. On the 21st of September he was made a full second-lieutenant. At the battle of Buena Vista he served on the staff of General Taylor, and for gallant and meritorious conduct in the action was breveted first-lieutenant in May, 1848, the commission bearing date February 23d, 1847.

In June, 1848, Lieutenant Franklin was ordered to West Point as assistant professor of natural and experimental philosophy, in which capacity he served until January, 1852. In February he was appointed professor of natural and experimental philosophy and civil engineering at the New York City Free Academy. In the same year he made a survey of Nag's Head and Roanoke Island, North Carolina, and in November was appointed engineer in charge of the harbor of Oswego, New York. He next held the office of lighthouse engineer and inspector on the coasts of Maine and New Hampshire, and superintendent of the erection of the custom-house and marine hospital at Portland, Maine. He was commissioned a full first-lieutenant in March, 1853, and captain on the 1st of July, 1857. In April, 1858, he was one of a board of engineers appointed to examine the mouth of Cape Fear River, North Carolina; in March, 1859, superintendent of the capitol and post-office extensions at Washington; in April, one of a board to report upon the Rock Island bridge, with reference to its obstruction of the Mississippi; and in March, 1861, superintendent of the extension of the national treasury buildings.

On the 14th of May, 1861, Captain Franklin was appointed colonel of the twelfth infantry, which had just been organized, and was ordered to New York to superintend the transportation of troops to the seat of war. On the 17th of the same month he was commissioned a brigadier-general of volunteers, and in July was assigned a brigade in Heintzelman's division of the army of Northeastern Virginia. At the battle of Bull Run he was "in the hottest of the fight," according to the official report of General McDowell, and was assigned the duty of covering the retreat.

Upon the reorganization of the army of the Potomac, in September, General Franklin was given the command of the first division of the first corps d'armée, consisting of Slocum's, Kearney's, and Newton's brigades. When McDowell was ordered to remain at Fredericksburg, Franklin was detached and sent to McClellan on the Peninsula. Transported by water to West Point, on York River, he there repulsed the enemy, under Generals Whiting and Smith, who attempted to prevent his landing, May 7th, 1862. On the 15th of the same month he was appointed to the command of the sixth corps d'armée.

He took part in the chief operations in front of Richmond; and during the movement to the James River, which began on the 27th of June, was charged with covering McClellan's retreat, repulsing the enemy on the right bank of the Chickahominy, June 27th and 28th, and again, in conjunction with General Sumner, at Savage's Station, June 29th. He commanded at the battle of White Oak Swamp Bridge on the 30th, holding the enemy in check all day, and silencing their batteries. The next day he rejoined the main body of the army at Harrison's Landing, on the James River. For his gallant and meritorious conduct in this campaign, the President, on the 4th of July, 1862, promoted him to the rank of brevet brigadier-general in the regular army and major-general of volunteers.

When McClellan was released from the Peninsula and ordered to reinforce Pope, he stopped at Acquia Creek, preventing Porter's and Franklin's corps from joining him. General Pope, deprived of this support, was virtually defeated, and on his arrival at Washington preferred charges against those generals; but, at the request of McClellan, the court martial was quashed by the President.

At South Mountain and Antietam, General Franklin commanded the reserve, and greatly distinguished himself by storming Crampton's Pass, which was held by the enemy in force and obstinately defended.

MAJOR-GENERAL PHILIP KEARNEY, U.S.V.

> "Fleet foot in the corrie, sage counsel in cumber,
> Red hand in the foray, how sound is thy slumber!
> Like the dew on the mountain, like the foam on the river,
> Like the bubble on the fountain, thou art gone, and forever!"

PHILIP KEARNEY was born in the city of New York on the 2d of June, 1815, during his mother's temporary sojourn there. In accordance with her wishes, he entered the law school of Columbia College; but the bar was not his destiny. His predilection was for the career of arms; and as soon as he became his own master, he entered the first regiment of dragoons, commanded by his uncle, Colonel S. W. Kearney, as second-lieutenant. Under his command he long fought the Indians with gallantry and success. In 1838 his distinction as a cavalry officer was such that he was sent to Europe by the Government to study and report upon the French cavalry tactics. He entered the Polytechnic School, and soon after joined the First Chasseurs d'Afrique as a volunteer, and greatly distinguished himself in the brilliant campaign of Marshal Vallée, which swept the Arabs from the plains of Metidjha, and forced the passage of the "Gates of Iron." His intrepidity and skill gained him exalted reputation, and the distinction of the Cross of the Legion of Honor.

Returning home in 1841, Kearney entered the Mexican War as captain of a company of dragoons, which he mounted and equipped at his own expense. This corps formed the escort of General Scott when he made his entrance into Vera Cruz. "For gallant and meritorious conduct" in the battles of Contreras and Churubusco, Captain Kearney was promoted to a majority. At the San Antonio gate of the city of Mexico he gave the order to charge a battery. A murderous volley checked his advance, and caused his troops to waver. Alone, with sword erect, Major Kearney dashed upon the enemy. Electrified by his example, his men followed their brave officer, and slaughtered the Mexicans at their guns. When he entered Mexico his left arm was gone.

After the Mexican War, Major Kearney was sent to California in command of an expedition against the Indians of the Columbia River, in which trying service his rare qualities as a bold, cool, brave commander shone out conspicuously. On the 9th of October, 1851, he resigned his commission, and returning to Europe, devoted several years to military studies. In 1859 occurred the Italian War, in which Major Kearney greatly distinguished himself, serving as volunteer aide to Marshal Maurice.

MAJOR-GENERAL PHILIP KEARNEY, U.S.V.

For his gallantry at Magenta and Solferino, the Emperor Napoleon bestowed upon him the Cross of the Legion of Honor.

When the news of the breaking out of the great rebellion first reached Europe, Major Kearney was residing in Paris. He lost not a moment, but hurried back to offer his services to his country. They were accepted, and the President appointed him a brigadier-general of volunteers from New Jersey on the 25th of July, 1861, his commission bearing date May 17th, 1861. The Senate confirmed his appointment on the 3d of August, and he was given the command of a brigade in the army of the Potomac. Wherever the advance was, there was Kearney. His vigilance was sleepless. Kearney, the "hero," the "ubiquitous," the "indomitable." These were the phrases in which he was continually spoken of, while from the enemy he received the flattering sobriquet of the "One-armed Devil!"

Throughout the bloody and disastrous campaign of the Peninsula his division was always in the hottest of the fight. When the seven days' battles occurred, he stayed last at his position, unwilling and almost refusing to go. He was bidden to leave his sick and wounded and retreat. He nevertheless brought every man of them away, and, covering the rear, he fought his way through, finishing at Malvern Hill the crowning conflict of that movement. In none of the battles was his fighting division repulsed, but held the field. In recognition of his great services in the Peninsula he received the commission of a major-general of volunteers.

No sooner did he join Pope, on Thursday, the 28th of August, than he was again in the advance and fighting. On Friday, the 29th, he drove the enemy from his position with heavy slaughter, leaving one thousand of his own dead and wounded, and holding his position all night and next day. During the retreat of some other troops, the division under Kearney remained in the field until ten o'clock at night, with the enemy in the rear, front, and on the right, and then retired in good order.

Chantilly wound up his great and glorious history. On Monday afternoon, September 1st, 1862, word came that the enemy were stealing in Pope's rear to cut him off from Washington. Reno's division was ordered to attack them. Kearney's had been fighting all the while before, but it was, nevertheless, ordered to support Reno. The firing became heavy. General Kearney was apprised by General Birney that Reno's troops had given way upon his left, and that there was a gap between their flanks which the enemy were occupying. He rode forward to see for himself if it could be so, telling his orderly and aides to keep back that he might be unnoticed. He left them, and did not return. The next morning, General Lee sent in a flag of truce with his body; and on Saturday, the 6th of September, his funeral took place at Trinity Church, New York, where his body rests, not far from that of the illustrious Montgomery. He was the Napoleon of the army—resembling him in his intuition, his power over men, his rapidity of execution, promptness of resolve, unflinching will—in every quality of that greatest of commanders. Yes, we may indeed mournfully ask, WHO CAN REPLACE PHILIP KEARNEY?

MAJOR-GENERAL A. DOUBLEDAY, U. S. V.

"The fame which a man wins for himself is best; —
That he may call his own."

ABNER DOUBLEDAY was born in the village of Ballston Spa, Saratoga county, New York, June 26th, 1819. His father, Ulysses F. Doubleday, who at that time edited the "Saratoga Sentinel," removed the same year to Auburn, New York, where he for many years published the "Cayuga Patriot," and was twice elected to Congress during General Jackson's administration. Abner early evinced a remarkable aptitude for study, and at the age of fourteen taught an evening class of his father's apprentices. Too much attention to books having injured his health, he obtained a position as civil engineer on the Utica and Schenectady Railroad, one of the first railroads constructed in the State. He was engaged subsequently on several other roads; and was in Canada, in 1838, employed in the survey of a route from Toronto to Lake Huron, during which he traversed both ways the almost unbroken wilderness, of nearly one hundred miles, between those two points. The insurrection of that year put a stop to the work, and he returned, with a constitution invigorated by out-door life, to Auburn, to find that he had been appointed a cadet at the West Point Military Academy, which he entered in September.

He graduated in June, 1842, in a class among whose members were Generals Rosecrans, Newton, Pope, Seth Williams, and Sykes of the United States army, and Van Dorn, Gustavus W. Smith, Lovell, Longstreet, Reins, and R. H. Anderson of the rebel army. He was commissioned at once as brevet second-lieutenant in the third artillery, and assigned to duty at Charleston, where Bragg was at that time serving as a lieutenant in the same company. In 1845 he was promoted second-lieutenant in the first artillery, and sailed in the fall of that year from New York for Corpus Christi, where General Taylor was assembling a force for the defence of Texas. In April of 1846 his company followed the army to Point Isabel; was left there when General Taylor advanced to opposite Matamoras, and took no part in the battles of Palo Alto and Resaca de la Palma. Finding that there was no chance of seeing service while he remained in that company, Lieutenant Doubleday applied to be exchanged into another. In this he succeeded, and was one of the famous artillery battalion which did such efficient service at the siege of Monterey. Lieutenant Doubleday's conduct attracted the notice, and received the commendation of his commanding officers.

In March, 1847, Lieutenant Doubleday was promoted to be first-lieutenant. In November, 1848, he returned to New York, and remained there until 1851—"Stonewall" Jackson being second-lieutenant in his company—when he was sent to Baltimore. Beauregard was stationed in the same fort with him. In 1852 he was married to Miss Mary Hewitt of Washington. In 1856 he was ordered to Florida, where he was actively engaged in the campaigns against the Seminoles.

In 1858 he was stationed at Fort Moultrie, Charleston Harbor, and, even at that early period, clearly saw the coming storm of secession. He was the first officer who crossed from Fort Moultrie to Fort Sumter. He never acquiesced in the do-nothing policy, by which the South Carolinians were allowed to build batteries and occupy important points under the guns of Sumter. When the "Star of the West" attempted to enter, and was fired on by the rebels, he made urgent request to be allowed to answer their batteries, and thus aid the troops sent to succor the little garrison. When the bombardment took place, he fired the first gun at the rebel works—the first gun fired on the side of the Union in this war.

In June he received his commission as major of the seventeenth infantry, dated May 14th, 1861. He served as commander of a heavy battery during Patterson's campaign, at the close of which he was put on duty in Washington, where, until his appointment as brigadier-general, February 3d, 1862, he was engaged in supplying the works on the south side of the Potomac with ammunition. As brigadier his first command consisted of the forts on the north side of the river. In May he joined General McDowell's corps at Fredericksburg, and was for a time in command of the forces left there when that general marched to attack Jackson.

He joined General Pope at Cedar Mountain in the middle of August, and with his brigade shared in the artillery combats at Rapahannock Station and Warrenton Sulphur Springs. On the 28th of August, at the battle of Groveton, by his quick decision and cool daring, with a small force he repulsed a large body of Longstreet's troops. So murderous was the enemy's fire that one-third of our men engaged fell in a fight of only forty-five minutes. The next day his men were again engaged at Manassas, and suffered severely. On Saturday, the 30th, though only able to muster five hundred men, his brigade behaved nobly, and was finally left so far alone that one of our own batteries fired on them, taking them for rebels, because they were so far in advance.

At South Mountain, after the gallant General Hatch had been wounded, General Doubleday assumed command of the division, and, after a fight for some time at a distance of only forty paces from the rebels, ordered his troops to cease firing. The enemy, thinking our line broken, rushed forward, but, at fifteen paces, were met by a deadly discharge, which sent them routed far to the rear. At Antietam his division was the only one engaged which was not driven back by the enemy. In the words of one on the field, whose report was universally copied, "Doubleday, on the right, inflexibly held his own."

Daniel Butterfield

MAJOR-GENERAL DANIEL BUTTERFIELD, U.S.V.

> "On his bold visage middle age
> Had slightly pressed its signet sage;
> Yet had not quenched the open truth,
> And fiery vehemence of youth;
> Forward and frolic glee was there,
> The will to do, the soul to dare."

DANIEL BUTTERFIELD was born in Utica, Oneida county, New York, October 31st, 1830. His father, John Butterfield, is at the head of the American Express Company, which has its agents domiciled in the remotest corners of the Continent. The son, Daniel, graduated at Union College, Schenectady, in the year 1849, and in 1851 received from that institution the degree of A.M. The good business habits instilled by the father found root, and Daniel entered his father's establishment in a prominent position.

In February, 1857, he was married to the accomplished eldest daughter of Edgar M. Brown of New York.

He early manifested a fondness for military pursuits, and became an earnest student of that science, and finally an active participant of its more practical duties. The breaking out of the rebellion found him in command of the Twelfth Regiment New York State Militia; and no sooner was the blast of treason sounded in his ears than he exchanged his peaceful occupations for the perilous but patriotic service of his country. Early in March, 1861, he hastened to Washington to tender his services to the Government, and obtained the permission of the Secretary of War to reorganize, fill up, and report his regiment at Washington on the 26th, prepared for duty. With this order, Colonel Butterfield made his way through Baltimore, wet with the gore of Northern citizens, and, over broken bridges and torn-up tracks, arrived in New York on Thursday night of the 20th, filled up his regiment (like most of our militia organizations then, merely a skeleton) from some three hundred and fifty to a thousand men, and left with them on Sunday afternoon in the "Baltic" for Washington, by the way of Fortress Monroe, looking to a passage up the Potomac, and then, by information there obtained, to Annapolis. Assigned to the army corps of Patterson on the 6th of July, the Twelfth saw their hopes of active service disappear in dreary marches and countermarches over the "sacred soil," while Bull Run was being fought, and the vanity of the South in arms supplied with material for boasting. In Patterson's division, General Butterfield, then lieutenant-colonel of the twelfth United

States infantry by a recent appointment, commanded a brigade, and sought for permission to lead it into action. Soon afterwards, September 7th, 1861, he received the appointment of brigadier-general of volunteers in an unsolicited and gratifying manner. During the autumn and winter, General Butterfield was profoundly occupied in drilling and disciplining his brigade, and converting them into those "stolid mud-sill veterans" so much deprecated by the South.

In the movement before Yorktown, General Fitz John Porter's command was always prominently engaged, and generally in the advance. Butterfield's brigade made the first reconnoissance to Big Bethel and Harold's Mill, and was with Porter when he made his first approaches and attack on Yorktown. On the 11th of April, a portion of the brigade repulsed a sortie of the enemy, receiving high encomiums from General Porter. At the battle of Hanover, on the first sound of firing, General Butterfield left his sick-bed for the saddle, and on receiving the order to advance, pushed his brigade forward in two lines; the seventeenth New York and the eighty-third Pennsylvania in the first, and the twelfth New York and the sixteenth Michigan in the second, these last in double column. Knowing, from the heavy firing in the front, that he was wanted, he advanced on the double quick. With skirmishers thrown out, they dashed though the wood, halting on its edge for a moment only to dress their line and reconnoitre the enemy, and then forward into the wheatfield adjoining, in splendid style, driving the enemy before them. Here the seventeenth New York captured one of the enemy's guns, a brass twelve-pounder.

Pushing on in the same order, they occupied the station of the Baltimore and Ohio Railroad and Hanover Court-house, which had never witnessed so much activity since its bricks were brought from England in 1735. At the Court-house the news reached them that the enemy had reappeared in their rear and threatened the left flank. General Martindale gallantly met and sustained this attack with but little more than two regiments, and a section of Martin's battery. This was one of the severest contested fights of the whole war, the enemy coming up boldly to the work, and showing themselves in a comparatively open field. Butterfield, led by the sound of the firing, was soon double-quicking back his weary men to the relief of one of his regiments, the forty-fourth New York, which was already warmly engaged supporting a section of Martin's battery; and arriving on the field with the eighty-third Pennsylvania on the enemy's flank, poured in a murderous fire, and the combined forces soon routed the enemy.

Again, at the battles of Mechanicsville and Gaines' Mills, General Butterfield won glory by his skill and bravery. The Prince de Joinville was so struck by his gallantry that he presented him with a horse in token of his regard.

General Butterfield's gallantry and good conduct went neither unnoticed nor unrewarded. In November, 1862, the President promoted him to the rank of major-general in the volunteer forces of the United States.

MAJOR-GENERAL I. I. STEVENS, U. S. V.

> "And is he gone?—the pure of the purest;
> The hand that upheld our bright banner the surest,
> Is he gone from our struggle away?
> But yesterday lending a people new life,
> Cold, mute in the coffin to-day!"

ISAAC INGALLS STEVENS was born in Andover, Massachusetts, in the year 1816. In 1835, young Stevens entered the West Point Military Academy, where he graduated in 1839, and was commissioned a second-lieutenant of engineers. Not only did he stand at the head of his class, but there were fifteen degrees in the scale of merit between him and the cadet next below him. On leaving West Point, Lieutenant Stevens was employed for several years in superintending the construction of sea-coast fortifications.

When the Mexican War broke out, he was detailed to duty on the staff of General Scott, and was with him from Vera Cruz to Mexico. "For gallant and meritorious conduct" in the battles of Contreras and Churubusco he was breveted captain; and his heroic courage in the storming of Chapultepec won for him the brevet of major. In the assault on the San Cosmo gate of the city of Mexico he received a severe gunshot wound in the foot, from which he suffered for many years.

On his return from Mexico, Major Stevens was chosen by Professor Bache, as chief of the Coast Survey Office at Washington. While there, Major Stevens also published a history, or rather criticism, of the Mexican War. This work is eminently philosophical, and displays a profound comprehension of strategic principles.

When the Government instituted the surveys and explorations for a route for the great Pacific railway, to Stevens was committed the most northerly survey contemplated, reaching from the head-waters of the Mississippi to Puget Sound. Stevens, at the solicitation of several eminent men, was also named governor of Oregon Territory, and ex-officio commissioner of Indian Affairs in his Territory. He detailed Captain McClellan to the western section of the survey, while he personally, accompanied by Captain Lander as a pioneer, superintended the eastern section.

After the completion of this work, the governor made treaties with the formidable Blackfeet, the Gros Ventres, the Pena Oreilles, and nearly twenty other tribes, and established friendly relations with twenty thousand Indians. Meanwhile, the Indians on the coast declared war. With difficulty, but with intrepid daring, Governor Stevens subdued the Indians, and saved the territories of Oregon and Washington. President

Pierce removed him, but the people of Washington Territory showed their appreciation of his services by electing him to Congress, where he again displayed his practical efficiency by securing, against the most violent opposition, the assumption by Congress of the war debt of Washington and Oregon. In 1860 he was chairman of the National Breckinridge Committee; but his whole career has shown how little he knew or sympathized with the traitorous schemes of that unhappy man.

When the great Southern rebellion broke out in the winter of 1860-'61, he denounced his recent political associates of the South, and urged President Buchanan to remove Floyd and Thompson, and crush incipient treason in the bud.

Hearing of the fall of Sumter in his distant home, he instantly started for Washington, and arriving there about the time of the battle of Bull Run, tendered his services to the Government. He was placed in command of the Seventy-ninth Regiment of N. Y. S. M. (Highlanders), made vacant by the fall of Colonel Cameron. The regiment, composed of magnificent fighting material, required the care of a thorough military mind to bring the men into good order and efficiency. Under Stevens' leadership they performed a service written over with glorious deeds. Ere long he was appointed brigadier-general, but never parted from his regiment. Together they went to Port Royal, and served in South Carolina until the defeat of Benham at James Island, where the Highlanders suffered severely. Soon after the Highlanders were returned to Washington, to partake once more in the defence of the capital. It was in this service that Stevens was killed.

The army was retreating from Centreville on the 1st of September. General Stevens' division, the advance of Reno's corps, was on the left of the road taken by the trains, and intercepted by the enemy. He saw that the rebels must be beaten back at once, or during the night they would stampede the wagons, and probably so disconcert our retreat that the last division would fall a prey to their main force. He decided to attack immediately, at the same time sending back for support.

Having made his dispositions, he led the attack on foot, at the head of the Seventy-ninth (Highlanders). Soon meeting a withering fire, and the color-sergeant being wounded, they faltered. One of the color guard took up the flag, when the general snatched it from him. The wounded Highlander at his feet cried, "For God's sake, general, don't *you* take the colors; they'll shoot you if you do!" The answer was, "Give me the colors! If they don't follow now, they never will;" and he sprung forward, crying, "We are all Highlanders; follow, Highlanders; forward, my Highlanders!" The Highlanders did follow their chief, but, while sweeping forward, a ball struck him on the right temple. He died instantly. An hour afterwards, when taken up, his hands were still clinched around the flag-staff.

Thus perished an admirable man, and an efficient officer—one whom the Republic, in this her trial hour, can but illy spare. Modest in mien, quiet in demeanor, and reticent of speech, he was resolute in will, heroic in conduct, and insensible to fear.

MAJOR-GENERAL CARL SCHURZ, U. S. V.

> "Earth may hide, waves ingulf, fire consume us,
>   But they shall not to slavery doom us:
> If they rule, it shall be o'er our ashes and graves;
>   But we've smote them already with fire on the waves,
> And new triumphs on land are before us:
>   To the charge! Heaven's banner is o'er us."

CARL SCHURZ was born in Bonn, on the Rhine, in the year 1828. He was educated at the University of Bonn, where he was the pupil and friend of the celebrated German poet, Godfrey Kinkel. He graduated there in 1848, just before the Revolution, when the tocsin of liberty rang through the land, and all noble minds were drawn into its vortex. Carl Schurz was among the foremost to offer his services to the good cause, and General Sigel appointed him upon his staff, with the rank of captain in the army of Baden. He was in every battle, and distinguished himself greatly by his skill and undaunted bravery. Where Sigel was, there was Schurz, and both seemed ubiquitous in the battle smoke. He was one of the defenders of the fortress of Rastadt; and when that stronghold surrendered to the Prussians, he was taken prisoner, and would have been condemned to death, had he not effected his escape from prison by one of those mysterious accidents which may really be called providential.

His old professor, Godfrey Kinkel, was also captured and condemned to death; but in consequence of the outcry of the whole nation against this cruel act, the king commuted his sentence to imprisonment for life. In 1850, Carl Schurz, in disguise, went from Paris to Berlin, and thence to Spandsau, where Kinkel was held prisoner in a dreadful dungeon, and by great personal risk and perseverance effected his escape, and tutor and scholar fled to England. The friends of freedom throughout the civilized world applauded this brave and chivalric deed; and from that moment Carl Schurz was the favorite of his countrymen.

In London he married Miss Margaretha Meyer, a gifted and accomplished lady, still the companion of his life.

In the year 1852 he emigrated to this country, and after a short stay in Philadelphia he went West, and settled in Watertown, Jefferson county, Wisconsin. Here his genius soon made itself known and felt, and he was honored by the State in the highest manner. In the presidential campaign of 1856, Carl Schurz arrayed himself, as ever, on the side of freedom and the cause of Fremont, both with tongue and pen. His speeches delivered in this campaign are among the finest of their kind. In the campaign of 1860 he again greatly aided the Republican cause by his fervid eloquence, and perhaps contributed more to the success of Mr. Lincoln's election than any other man, by arraying on his side the entire German vote of the West.

After the inauguration of Mr. Lincoln, he appointed Mr. Schurz the minister plenipotentiary to Spain on the 1st of May, 1861, and he was received at Madrid with the greatest honors. The battle of Bull Run, however, brought him back again in February; and expressing his great desire to enter the field, the President appointed him a brigadier-general of volunteers on the 15th of April, 1862. He was immediately given the command of a brigade, and afterwards of the third division of the first corps d'armée, General Sigel.

With this command he went through the fiery ordeal of Pope's campaign in Virginia. He fought gallantly and well on the Rapidan, on the Rappahannock, at Cedar Mountain, at Groveton, and Bull Run. At the latter battle he particularly distinguished himself, and won the encomiums of his great leader. On the first day, August 29th, Schurz' division, went into action at five o'clock in the morning, mostly without breakfast, and fought most bravely against superior numbers until two o'clock P. M., when, their ammunition being exhausted, and being decimated by enormous losses, they were relieved by some regiments kindly sent by General Hooker. In the next day's battle the division formed a general reserve. They were, however, under a heavy fire of shot and shell nearly all day until dark, when the enemy's fire suddenly ceased. The time had now arrived for a vigorous attack on our part, which would probably have met with entire success; but General Pope had given the order to retreat to Centreville. Schurz' division formed the rear guard, and arrived at Centreville at seven the next morning, after a bivouac of two hours. Their loss in this bloody contest, which exceeded twenty per cent. of the whole effective force, shows how bravely they fought and bled.

MAJOR-GENERAL JOSEPH K. F. MANSFIELD, U. S. V.

> "Hang out our banners on the outward walls;
> The cry is still, 'They come!' Our castle's strength
> Will laugh a siege to scorn."

JOSEPH K. FENNO MANSFIELD was the youngest child of Mary Fenno and Henry S. Mansfield, and was born at New Haven, on the 22d of December, 1803. At the age of fourteen he received a cadet's appointment, and entered the military academy at West Point, where he gave early promise of his future greatness. Young Mansfield graduated July 1st, 1822, a youth of nineteen, the youngest in years and the second in rank. Immediately after, he received a commission in the corps of Engineers, and became a brevet second lieutenant.

From 1826 to 1828 he acted as assistant engineer, in the construction of Fort Hamilton, at the Narrows. For the next two years he was similarly engaged in the building of Forts Monroe and Calhoun, at Old Point Comfort. Fort Pulaski, at the mouth of the Savannah River, is a monument of his labors and genius as an architect. For these, and many other high professional services, Lieutenant Mansfield became a captain of engineers, in 1838.

Throughout the Mexican war, he was the chief engineer of General Taylor, and possessed his fullest respect and confidence. Arriving at Point Isabel, General Taylor ordered Mansfield to plan its defence. In half a day the ground was surveyed, the key to the position determined, a redoubt traced to cover it, and he joined his commander at Matamoras, where he was ordered to erect a battery to command the town and construct a fort to hold the position. The main army now fell back on Point Isabel. With his garrison weak, his works unfinished, his materials to be brought from points miles away, he must show that he can not only build forts, but defend them. The storm soon came. "Threatened in rear by light troops, bombarded in front by heavy batteries, day and night the devoted garrison fought and labored, and the army, as it came, shattered and bleeding, but victorious, from the plains of Palo Alto and Resaca de la Palma, saw the loved flag of the Union still flying defiant over the little garrison of Fort Brown." For his distinguished conduct in its defence, during a bombardment of a week, Captain Mansfield was breveted a major.

The next advance of the army was on Monterey, where, on the second day, Major Mansfield was ordered to make a forced reconnoissance of the enemy's redoubt on the left, and take it if possible. The order was executed and the redoubt taken in fine

MAJOR-GENERAL JOSEPH K. F. MANSFIELD, U. S. V.

style. Early in the battle he was shot through the leg, but he still kept at his work all that day and part of the next, when his wounds compelled him to retire, and prostrated him for six weeks. But he did not go unrewarded. The major became a lieutenant-colonel, and the battle of Buena Vista found him again ready for action. This contest began on the 22d of February, 1847, and lasted two days. Colonel Mansfield spent all the first day in reconnoitering the enemy and the mountain-passes, and by order of General Wool remained all night on the ground, while General Taylor returned to Saltillo. The next morning the enemy renewed the fight with great spirit, defeating and putting to flight our left. At this moment, Lieutenant-Colonel Mansfield rode forward, and, assuming command, brought up Colonel Key's reserve regiment, formed a new line, on which the unbroken troops fell back, formed anew, and saved the battle. For his services and gallantry, he was promoted to the rank of colonel.

At the close of the war, Colonel Mansfield was assigned to duty at the fortifications at Boston Harbor, became a member of the board of engineers, and in 1853, was appointed inspector-general of the army. In this high capacity he inspected the department of New Mexico once, and California and Texas twice, and had just returned from the latter field when he was appointed a brigadier-general of the regular army of the United States on the 14th of May, 1861, and was summoned to the defence of Washington. Here, when the capital was filled with traitors and weak with fear, General Mansfield fortified the city on every side, took possession of Arlington Heights and Alexandria, and by his iron will, sleepless energy, and constant industry, protected the nation's heart when its life-beats seemed almost destined to cease.

General Mansfield was then put successively in command of Forts Monroe, Hatteras, Camp Hamilton, and Newport News, at which latter place he saved the Congress from the sad yet glorious fate of the Cumberland, and took part in the Norfolk expedition on the 10th of May, 1862. When McClellan entered upon his Maryland campaign, in the fall, General Mansfield was assigned to the command of a corps which he led most gallantly through the battle of South Mountain, on the 14th of September, defeating and driving the enemy wherever he met them. Following Lee to Antietam, Hooker was sent across the creek on the afternoon of the 16th, supported by General Mansfield's corps, and renewed the attack at daybreak on the 17th. Mansfield promptly brought up his command, and while assisting in driving back the enemy, was pierced by a ball, and fell, as the gallant old hero would have wished to, at the head of his brave and victorious troops; and the President paid a fitting tribute to his fame and services by issuing a major-general's commission bearing his name and the date of that memorable action.

MAJOR-GENERAL J. A. GARFIELD, U. S. V.

> "For our boys that knew not fear;
> For their 'gallant Brigadier;'
> For their leader, brave and young;
> For their praise on every tongue!
> *Te laudamus, Domine!*"

JAMES ABRAM GARFIELD is one of the youngest generals in the army of the Union. He was born in Cuyahoga county, Ohio, in November, 1831. Being left fatherless while yet a child, he early learned the lessons of labor and self-reliance. In 1856 he graduated at Williams College, Mass., and was immediately afterwards employed as a teacher of Latin and Greek in the Eclectic Institute at Hiram, Ohio, his present place of residence. In 1857 he was elected to the presidency of the institution, which position he held till the breaking out of the war. In 1859 he was elected to the Ohio Senate, where he served for two years, and was an acknowledged leader in all the bold and decisive measures which attended and followed the breaking out of hostilities.

In September, 1861, he was appointed colonel of the Forty-second Regiment Ohio Volunteers, and raised a large part of the regiment himself, one company being almost wholly composed of his own students.

On the 17th of December he was called to Louisville, and put in command of an expedition, with orders to drive General Humphrey Marshall, with his rebel force of five thousand men, from Eastern Kentucky. Ordering a regiment of infantry and four hundred cavalry to march from Paris, Kentucky, toward Prestonburg, he hastened to the mouth of the Big Sandy, which he reached on the 22d of December, and advanced up the valley with two regiments of infantry and a squadron of cavalry. Marshall occupied the village of Paintville, sixty miles from the mouth of the river, and was strongly fortified. By a series of bold and rapid manœuvres, Colonel Garfield misled the enemy as to his own strength and intentions; and after a dashing cavalry fight near Paintville, in which the rebels lost twenty-five in killed and wounded, Marshall destroyed a large quantity of his stores and retreated precipitately from his intrenchments, and Colonel Garfield took possession while the camp fires were still burning. On the same day he was joined by the column from Paris. Sending his cavalry to harass the enemy's rear, he set out with eleven hundred men to intercept Marshall's retreat, and compel him to fight. On the 10th of January, 1862, he overtook and attacked his main force, posted on a semicircle of precipitous hills, near Prestonburg, and, after five hours' desperate fighting, completely routed him, killing one hundred, and taking many prisoners and stores, but losing less than thirty of his own men. Marshall fled during the night, and soon crossed the mountains into Virginia. This was the first of those brilliant victories which made the campaign in the West illustrious. Colonel Garfield received the thanks of the Legislatures of Ohio and Kentucky, and was immediately made brigadier-general, his commission taking date from the day of the battle. The following general order was issued in reference to his campaign: "The General Commanding takes occasion to thank Colonel Garfield and his troops for their successful campaign against the rebel force under General Marshall on the Big Sandy, and their gallant conduct in battle. They have overcome formidable difficulties in the character of the country, the condition of the roads, and the inclemency of the season; and, without artillery, have in several engagements, terminating with the battle of Middle Creek on the 10th instant, driven the enemy from his intrenched positions, and forced him back into the mountains with the loss of a large amount of baggage and stores, and many of his men killed or captured. These services have called into action the highest qualities of a soldier—fortitude, perseverance, courage."

He soon after pushed on to Piketon, one hundred miles from the mouth of the river, and captured or dispersed the guerilla bands which infested that part of the State. Pound Gap, a pass through the Cumberland Mountains, forty miles above Piketon, was strongly fortified and held by a garrison of five hundred rebels. After a rapid march of two days, General Garfield reached the foot of the mountain, March 16th, and sending his cavalry to advance along the road leading to the pass and engage the enemy's attention, he led his infantry in person up the mountain by a steep and unfrequented path, and, amidst a furious snow-storm, attacked and routed the rebels, capturing and burning sixty log huts and a large quantity of stores.

Toward the close of March he was ordered to join General Buell, and commanded the twentieth brigade in the battle of Shiloh. He took a prominent part in the fighting at Corinth, and in all the subsequent operations in northern Alabama. He has lately been ordered to Washington to take a position in the army of the East. In the fall of 1862, General Garfield was chosen, without solicitation on his part, to represent the people of the nineteenth district of Ohio in the next Congress, where he will make his mark.

General Garfield is an earnest Christian; and, though not an ordained minister, he has often spoken in the pulpit of the church to which he belongs. He believes that whatever ought to be done, it is a Christian's duty to do, and that religion does not make men timid and inefficient, but stronger for all great, earnest work. He is a man of decided energy, and iron will; quick to determine, and bold to execute. He inspires his soldiers with unbounded confidence and enthusiasm. His fellow-citizens have just reason to expect for him a useful and brilliant future.

MAJOR-GENERAL JACOB DOLSON COX, U.S.V.

"Suaviter in modo, fortiter in re."

JACOB DOLSON COX was born at Montreal, October 27th, 1828. His parents, natives of New York city, resided at the former city about five years, while his father was engaged in the construction of the Catholic cathedral at that place, of which he was the architect. It was during this temporary residence that General Cox was born. At the age of eighteen, young Cox was sent to Oberlin College, Ohio, to complete his education, finishing the course of study prescribed in that institution during the winter of 1849-50. During the same year, he married a daughter of Rev. C. G. Finney, President of the College, and in 1851 moved to Warren, Ohio, his present residence, where he soon after entered upon the practice of law, in which profession he won a high and enviable position.

In 1859, he was chosen to the Senate of Ohio. During the session of 1860-61, he was foremost to urge preparation for the conflict, which his sure prescience satisfied him could not be long delayed, and was regarded as the leader of the war party.

Upon the breaking out of the rebellion, Cox was called by Governor Dennison to assist in the organization of the military of the State. While thus engaged, he was thrown into close business relations with General McClellan, just appointed major-general of the Ohio forces, and an intimacy sprang up between them, which ripened into enduring regard, as was shown by his being afterward chosen by that officer, to take charge of the Kanawha Expedition.

The rank of brigadier-general was conferred upon him, on May 17th, 1861, and Camp Dennison fixed as his field of immediate operations, where he remained until the 4th of July, when with a new force, his own brigade having been sent to General McClellan's army, he started to clear the rebels from the Kanawha Valley. How promptly and efficiently this task was performed, is now a part of the history of the country. Entering the valley as General McClellan entered Northwestern Virginia, he drove the rebel General Wise, and his army, from point to point, until the strong position of Gauley Bridge was gained, and the pursuit arrested by orders from headquarters. When General Rosecrans renewed active operations, Cox held the most important position connected with the new plan of the campaign, and obtained the name of the fighting general of the army. When our forces were encamped at Sewell Mountain, with Floyd and Wise in their front, four other brigadiers voted against attacking them, while General Cox alone voted fight.

MAJOR-GENERAL JACOB DOLSON COX, U. S. V.

Condemned to inactivity by the policy that then forbade pushing for the East Tennessee Railroad, and breaking up the link from East to West, General Cox continued to discharge the less prominent, but equally responsible duty, of guarding the country he had won. Through the winter and spring, he held the lines against every rebel attempt until Fremont's campaign began. In the plans of that commander, his division was given a prominent part. As Fremont pushed over the Cheat Mountain range, Cox advanced up the New River as far as Princeton, and stood ready to coöperate in the dashing operations of the Commanding General. Suddenly Banks was driven down the Shenandoah Valley. Fremont gave up his own movements, and rushed to save the capital. The elevation of Pope, relieving Fremont from the chief command, the whole plan of the Mountain Department was abandoned, obliging Cox to cease offensive operations, and confine himself to holding the range of mountains known as Flat-top Mountain, near Princeton, at the same time keeping open the route for his supplies to the Ohio river.

From that position, the renewed distress at the capital, during the retreat of Pope from the Rappahannock, relieved him, and with a little over half his command, General Cox was hurriedly ordered forward to the East.

At South Mountain, his conduct received the warmest commendation from the commanding general, and upon the death of General Reno, he was placed in command of the 9th Army corps. At Antietam, he again displayed alike the most brilliant gallantry and marked ability, and the Ohio troops under his leadership won fresh laurels.

For the skill with which the 9th Corps was handled at Antietam, and the persistent bravery shown in storming the bridge across that creek, and gaining the Sharpsburg heights, General Cox was soon after promoted, by the President, to a major-generalship.

Meantime, taking advantage of General Cox's absence in the East, the rebels had made a dash at the remaining troops, in the neighborhood of Gauley, and driven them down to the mouth of the Kanawha; thus regaining possession of the entire valley, with its immense salt, and other mineral resources, the taking and holding of which had cost so much labor and patience. As soon as Lee's army had been driven across the Potomac, after the battle of Antietam, General Cox was again ordered West, and given the command of the department of Western Virginia, with a large force, composed in part of the remains of his old regiments. He assumed command of Western Virginia in the latter part of October.

General Cox is one of nature's noblemen. Affable in his manner, and pleasant in his address; always showing great tact and carefulness of the feelings of others; he is, nevertheless, when aroused, impetuous and irresistible as the whirlwind. In person he is tall and well-proportioned, with dark grey, magnetic eyes, and a voice that, when raised to command, rings like a clarion. He is now in the prime of manhood, and the star of his fame is in the ascendant.

MAJOR-GENERAL WILLIAM SPRAGUE, U.S.V.

"Non nobis sed pro patria."

WILLIAM SPRAGUE was born at Cranston, Rhode Island, on the 12th of September, 1830. At the age of fifteen he entered his uncle's factory in Cranston, in the retail department. At sixteen he was transferred to the counting-room of A. & W. Sprague, Providence, where he gradually advanced until he became a book-keeper. At the age of twenty-two he became an active participant in the concern. Four years after, when his uncle William died, he assumed the whole weight of the business. They own and have in operation nine cotton mills, the full capacity of which is eight hundred thousand yards per week; while their printing establishment, when in full operation, is capable of turning out twenty-five thousand pieces, or about one million yards of calico in the same time.

Mr. Sprague at an early age joined the Marine Artillery company in Providence, as a private. He was soon promoted to the rank of lieutenant, and then to that of captain, and finally its colonel. He took a great interest in this company, and spared neither time nor money to make it one of the most efficient batteries of light artillery in the country.

In 1859, he went to Europe. He visited all the battle-fields made memorable in the Italian war, became acquainted with Garibaldi, and made a liberal contribution to the fund which that patriot was then raising. On his return, he was nominated and elected Governor of Rhode Island by a large majority, and the following year, 1861, reëlected.

In February, 1861, when it appeared evident that the Southern States were bent on rebellion, Governor Sprague visited Washington, and tendered to General Scott and to President Lincoln a full regiment of infantry, and a battery of light artillery, in case they should be wanted, at the shortest notice.

Three days after the call of the President for 75,000 men was received, he dispatched the First Battery of Light Artillery, fully equipped; and two days later he accompanied the First Rhode Island regiment, twelve hundred strong, under Colonel Burnside, well armed and equipped, and provisioned for thirty days. After remaining a few weeks in Washington, he returned and exerted himself in raising a new regiment. While thus employed, the Rhode Island force at Washington was ordered to take the advance on Harper's Ferry. The governor immediately joined these troops, and went through the campaign at the head of the column, on foot, with the then colonel, now Major-General Burnside, by his side. The new regiment was soon formed, and with a second battery of artillery left for the Capital, under command of Colonel Slocum, accompanied by Governor Sprague.

The Rhode Island troops were among the foremost in the memorable battle of Bull Run, and suffered severely. No one was more prominent in the action than Governor Sprague. He was in the thickest of the fight, and when his horse was shot from under him, he seized a rifle from a dead soldier, and, rushing forward, took his place among the soldiers, encouraging them by his presence and bravery. Two bullet holes found in his clothes after the battle show that he did not shun danger. He returned to Rhode Island and raised three more regiments of infantry, ten full batteries of light artillery, and a regiment of cavalry.

On the occupancy of Manassas by our troops in March last, Governor Sprague at once proceeded to the battle-field of Bull Run, accompanied by some of the Rhode Island regiment who had been taken prisoners, and who knew where several officers who fell in the battle were buried. They succeeded in finding three of them, viz: Colonel Slocum, Major Ballou, and Captain Tower, whose remains were taken back to Rhode Island, and there buried. The governor then returned to Virginia, and joined the division of the grand army of the Potomac, under Major-General McClellan.

This vast army, it is well known, extended a great distance, and occupied a large extent of country; but Governor Sprague was, as usual, to be found where there was most to do, and hence where there was most danger. While reconnoitering before Yorktown, his aide-de-camp, Colonel Tristram Burges, received a dangerous wound. In the severe action at Williamsburg the governor took part. After reaching a point near Richmond with the advance, his official duties required his return to Rhode Island, to be installed as Governor of the State, to which office he had just been elected without opposition. The day after he was installed, May 29, he was, by the General Assembly, elected United States Senator for six years, from the 4th of March, 1863—receiving 92 votes out of the 103 cast. A few hours after the election, he again took his departure for Washington, accompanying two regiments, the Ninth and Tenth, which he organized and equipped in two days after receiving the telegraphic dispatch from the Secretary of War, that more troops were required for the defence of Washington.

Few men in the country have risen so rapidly from private life to the highest position in the gift of the people, next to that of the Presidency, as Governor Sprague.

Robert Anderson

BRIGADIER-GENERAL ROBERT ANDERSON, U.S.A.

> "I thought of Sumter all the night;
> Of those beleaguered few
> Who stood up nobly in the fight
> For loyalty and freedom's right,
> Against that recreant crew."

ROBERT ANDERSON was born in Kentucky, September, 1805. He entered the West Point Military Academy in 1821, and, graduating in 1825, he was commissioned a second-lieutenant of infantry. During the Black Hawk War, in 1832, he was Inspector-General of the Illinois volunteers, and the next year he was promoted to a first-lieutenancy, and became instructor and inspector at West Point. He became aide-de-camp to General Scott in 1838, and a few months afterwards published his book, "Instruction for Field Artillery, Horse and Foot; arranged for the Service of the United States." On the 2d of April, of the same year, Lieutenant Anderson received the brevet of captain, which was honorably earned by his gallantry in the Florida War. He afterwards served as assistant adjutant-general, having the rank of captain; but on being promoted to the captaincy of his own regiment, he relinquished the office in 1841.

He was actively engaged through the whole Mexican War. In the siege of Vera Cruz, he had command of one of the batteries, which was distinguished for the precision of its fire and its unceasing activity. He was severely wounded in the attack on El Molino del Rey, and his conduct is thus spoken of in the dispatches of Captain Blake: "Captain Robert Anderson (acting field officer) behaved with great heroism on this occasion. Even after receiving a severe and painful wound, he continued at the head of the column, regardless of pain and self-preservation, and setting a handsome example to his men of coolness, energy and courage." He was also highly spoken of in General Garland's report, not only as being among the first to force an entrance into the strong position of El Molino del Rey, but also for his gallant defence of the captured works. For his gallantry and intrepidity in this action, he was breveted major, September 8th, 1847. On the 8th of October, 1857, he was promoted to the majority of the First Regiment of Artillery, a position which he held on the breaking out of the infamous Slaveholders' Rebellion of 1861.

Early in December, 1860, Major Anderson was ordered to relieve Colonel Gardiner in command of Fort Moultrie, Charleston Harbor. On the 19th of that month, South Carolina seceded from the Union, and soon commenced hostile demonstrations. Moultrie was out of repair, garrisoned by only sixty men, reinforcements were denied them, and hostilities daily grew more imminent. On the night of the 26th of December, Major Anderson dismantled the fort, spiked its guns, and conveyed its garrison and stores to Fort Sumter— an octagonal, casemated fortress of great strength. This act, so necessary to his own preservation, greatly incensed the traitors, who declared it to be a hostile act, and clamored for his removal. Events drifted fast to a crisis, and civil war was at hand. The "Star of the West," with reinforcements for the fort, was fired on by the rebel batteries, and compelled to put back. At length the storm burst in all its fury on the heads of the devoted garrison.

On the 11th of April, General Beauregard demanded of Major Anderson the evacuation of the fort, which demand was not complied with. At half-past three o'clock the next morning, Major Anderson was notified that the batteries under command of General Beauregard would open on Fort Sumter in one hour. These batteries were armed with nearly 200 pieces of heavy ordnance, and manned by 7,000 men.

Accordingly, at half-past four o'clock, the first matricidal blow at the heart of the Union was struck. Fort Sumter continued silent, however, until seven o'clock, when the answering gun boomed forth. As the fire of the enemy became warm, it was found that every portion of the fort was exposed to the mortars, and shells burst in every direction. Cartridges soon gave out, and this with the absence of the necessary implements to point the guns, rendered an accurate fire impossible. At 6 P.M. Sumter's fire ceased, but that of the enemy was kept up all night, with a little cessation. At 7 o'clock the next morning, Sumter reopened her fire. An hour after, the officers' quarters caught fire, and the work of the guns was necessarily slackened. By noon, the whole roof of the barracks was in flames, the magazine emptied, and the doors closed : but as the fire spread, the powder had to be thrown overboard. The flag-staff was cut about one o'clock, and the flag was then nailed to the cut piece, and raised upon the ramparts. At this time, both officers and men were compelled to lie flat upon their faces, and hold wet cloths to their mouths, to avoid suffocation. At one o'clock P.M., the flag of Fort Sumter was drawn down, and the fort was surrendered on honorable terms.

On the 15th of April, Major Anderson evacuated Fort Sumter, and after saluting his flag, embarked for New York, where he arrived three days after, and met with a most enthusiastic reception. On the 22d, he received the thanks of the government for his conduct at Fort Sumter, and on the 24th of May, he was appointed a brigadier-general in the volunteer service of the United States. He was assigned to the Department of Kentucky, which he assumed the command of on the 21st of September, and issued a spirited proclamation, calling upon Kentuckians of all parties to assist in repelling the invaders of the State. But his health, so much impaired at Fort Sumter, soon failed him, and on the 8th of October, he relinquished his command and returned to New York.

In June, 1862, Major Anderson was made a colonel and brevet brigadier-general of the regular army of the United States.

BRIGADIER-GENERAL NATHANIEL LYON, U.S.V.

> "Rest, Patriot, in thy hill-side grave,
> Beside her form who bore thee!
> Long may the land thou died'st to save,
> Her bannered stars wave o'er thee!
> Upon her history's brightest page.
> And on Fame's glowing portal,
> She'll write thy grand, heroic rage,
> And grave thy name immortal!"

NATHANIEL LYON was born at Ashford, Connecticut, in June, 1819. He entered the United States Military Academy, at West Point, July 1st, 1837; graduated in 1841, and was appointed a second-lieutenant of infantry. He served in the Seminole War, and at different posts on the Western frontier, and was promoted, February, 1847, to be first-lieutenant. In the Mexican War, he served at the bombardment of Vera Cruz, the battle of Cerro Gordo, and was wounded in the assault on the Belen gate. "For gallant and meritorious conduct" in the battles of Conteras and Churubusco, he was breveted captain, August, 1848.

When the Mexican War was ended, Lyon was ordered to California, where he was employed against the Indians, for several years. The full rank of captain was conferred upon him, June 11, 1851. From California he was ordered to Kansas and Nebraska, where he served during the height of the political troubles there.

Captain Lyon was in command of the arsenal at St. Louis, when, on May 6th, 1861, the police commissioners of that city demanded the removal of the United States soldiers from all places occupied by them outside the arsenal grounds, which he refused to do. On the 10th of May, he surrounded and captured a body of rebels under the command of General Frost, at Camp Jackson. This quick and severe blow at treason in Missouri awakened great joy in the hearts of all loyal men, and four days later, when General Harney arrived at St. Louis and took command there, Captain Lyon was elected to the command of the first brigade of Missouri Volunteers. Being left in command of the department by the removal of General Harney on the 31st of May, General Lyon soon commenced active operations by marching against the so called State troops at Jefferson City. On his approach, Governor Jackson fled to Booneville, burning the bridges after him; but Lyon soon after came up with him, and, though Jackson's force was double his own, he totally defeated him and occupied Booneville the same day. General McCulloch was at this time in the southern part of the State, and was joined soon after by Generals Price, Parsons, and Rains. Nothing daunted by the great disparity of numbers, Lyon marched against them on the 3d of July. His small force swelled as he advanced, and when he reached Springfield, July 20th, his command numbered ten thousand men; but this force had again decreased to six thousand by the 1st of August. On that day General Lyon marched to look for the rebels, and the next, about noon, at a place called Dug Spring, met the enemy and defeated them. August 3d, the march was continued six miles further, but the enemy made no stand, and, unable to bring on a general action, and being out of provisions, and with many of his men ill, Lyon marched his force back to Springfield, which he reached on the 5th of August. McCulloch and Price followed with a force of twenty-four thousand men, and encamped at Wilson's Creek, ten miles south of Springfield, August 6th. General Lyon, thus vastly outnumbered, had no resource but to attack them. He accordingly marched from Springfield at sunset, on the 9th, with but little over five thousand men, disposed in two columns. The first, under General Lyon in person, attacked the rebels about five, A.M., and drove them from an eminence, on which he immediately posted the artillery and opened fire. Repeated attempts of the rebels to carry this position were repulsed. Colonel Sigel, at the head of the second column, made his attack in the rear and fired their baggage train, when the battle was virtually relinquished.

From the first attack General Lyon had actively assisted and encouraged his men where the fight was thickest, and was thrice wounded. Near nine, A.M., when the enemy were about to make one of their attempts against Totten's battery, the first Iowa regiment was brought up to support it. This regiment had lost its colonel, and when Lyon ordered it to repel the enemy with the bayonet, the men called upon him to lead them. He mounted his horse to lead the charge, and gave the word. The rebels did not stand, but delivered their fire and broke. General Lyon was struck by a rifle ball in the breast; he fell into the arms of his body-servant and expired almost immediately. The battle went on, though its leader had fallen. Few of either officers or men knew what had occurred. The enemy being repulsed, returned with fresh regiments, again and again, but returned only to retreat in confusion, leaving their trail strewn with the fallen. Our troops advanced and took possession of the field. The rebels, in fear, now burned their own baggage wagons. Volumes of smoke rolled up from every side of the battle field, and concentrating above them, hung the heavens in a drapery of mourning.

BRIGADIER-GENERAL GEORGE A. McCALL, U.S.V.

"But the Philistines took him, and brought him down to Gaza."

GEORGE ARCHIBALD McCALL was born in Philadelphia on the 16th of March, 1802, and was educated in the public schools of the "City of Brotherly Love." In 1818 he entered the United States Military Academy at West Point, and graduated in 1822, receiving a commission as second-lieutenant in the first regiment of infantry. In January, 1829, he was promoted to the rank of first-lieutenant, and appointed assistant commissary of subsistence in the latter part of the same year, and in the same year was transferred to the fourth regiment of infantry. In 1831, General Gaines selected him as one of his aides-de-camp. He served in this capacity, and as assistant adjutant-general of the Western Department, till September, 1836, when he was promoted to the rank of captain. When the Florida War broke out, his company was ordered there, and served with distinction against the Indians. So gallant was Captain McCall's conduct in the battle of Pelahlikaha that General Worth strongly recommended him for a major's brevet; which, however, was not conferred.

In the Mexican War, Captain McCall was breveted major "for gallant and meritorious conduct" on the field of Palo Alto, and lieutenant-colonel at the battle of Resaca de la Palma. On his return, his bravery was acknowledged by the citizens of Philadelphia, who presented him with a sword. On the 7th of July, 1846, he was appointed assistant adjutant-general, which staff appointment he retained until promoted, on the 22d of December, 1847, to the majority of the third regiment of infantry. In June, 1850, President Taylor appointed Major McCall inspector-general of the army, with the rank of colonel of cavalry. On account of ill health he resigned his commission, April 29th, 1853, and retired to his residence in Chester county, Pennsylvania.

On the breaking out of the great slaveholders' rebellion in 1861, Governor Curtin authorized Colonel McCall to organize a corps of fifteen thousand men, to be called the "Pennsylvania Volunteer Reserve Corps." He obeyed the summons with alacrity, and in two months marched into Washington at the head of this fine corps. It was converted into a division, and McCall having been appointed a brigadier-general in the volunteer service of the United States on the 17th of May, 1861, joined the army of the Potomac with his command. During the next six months they occupied the post of danger, six to ten miles west of Washington.

On the 20th of December, 1861, the rebels, under General Stuart, made a foray near Dranesville, Virginia; General McCall, expecting it, marched out to give them

BRIGADIER-GENERAL GEORGE A. McCALL, U. S. V.

battle. Stuart took up a strong position on the Dranesville Heights; but, after a well-contested action of an hour and a half, he was routed, and fled in disorder.

On the 24th of June, 1862, McCall's division, forming part of McDowell's corps d'armée, joined McClellan on the Peninsula. Two days later he was attacked at Mechanicsville by the rebel general, Lee, with fourteen thousand men. McCall's position was a strong one, and bravely was it defended. It was attacked repeatedly and determinedly by the rebels, but each time they were driven back with terrible slaughter, until night's dark mantle closed over the scene. At daylight the next morning, General McCall was ordered to fall back five miles, to Gaines' Mills; and difficult as the movement was, in the face of the enemy, it was executed with great success. The same afternoon the rebels, reinforced to fifty thousand men, pressed hard upon Porter's corps of twenty-two thousand, and compelled him to fall back across the Chickahominy after a hard fight of four hours. In this severe conflict General McCall received great praise from the commanding general.

On the 30th of June, his division, reduced to six thousand men, was required to defend McClellan's immense wagon train at the New Market Road, against Lee's force of twenty thousand men. The odds were terrible, but retreat was impossible; so, fighting desperately, he maintained his position with immense loss, and secured the safe passage of the train. At the close of the day, having silenced the rebel's fire on the left and centre, General McCall brought up his reserve of five hundred men to oppose them on the right. The night was dark, and of his personal escort but two remained. Halting the reserve, he rode forward to ascertain whether any of his men were still in the front, and, in the darkness, found himself surrounded and a prisoner.

He was kept in prison and in close confinement at Richmond for six weeks, when he was exchanged, and returned to his home in Chester county to recover his health, which had been so sadly impaired by his imprisonment. He soon recovered his wonted vigor, and is ready for active service.

BRIGADIER-GENERAL FREDERICK W. LANDER, U.S.V.

> "The hand of the reaper takes the ears that are hoary,
> But the voice of the weeper wails manhood in glory;
> The autumn winds rushing waft the leaves that are serest,
> But our flower was in flushing when blighting was nearest."

FREDERICK W. LANDER was a native of Salem, Massachusetts, and belonged to a family eminent for genius and enterprise. He was not a graduate of any military academy, but was engaged in civil life up to the time of the breaking out of the present rebellion, being by profession an engineer. In 1859 and 1860, he was the Superintendent of the Overland Wagon Road to California, and carried on his operations on the great plains with extraordinary energy and skill. In this work he was greatly molested by the Indians, and he got up an expedition against the savages, which resulted in their complete pacification, and in which he himself displayed the highest qualities of coolness and courage. What our infantry with their discipline and steel could not accomplish, Lander achieved—the entire subjugation of the Indians of that section, and their obedience to the government.

Soon after his return he was brought prominently before the public as the second of the Hon. John F. Potter, when he was challenged by that pink of Virginian chivalry, Roger A. Pryor. By his judicious management of that case he enabled Mr. Potter to vindicate the representatives of the North against the braggarts of the South. When Pryor declined to fight Potter with Bowie knives, Lander politely offered to espouse the cause of his principal, and give the Virginian the choice of any weapon he pleased, but Pryor discreetly declined. This affair put a stop to the insolence of the chivalry in the United States House of Representatives for some time, and taught them to mend their plantation manners.

When the Southern rebellion broke out, Colonel Lander threw himself into the struggle in behalf of the Union, and was detailed to Western Virginia, under General McClellan. There he participated with Colonel Kelly in the attack on Phillipi on the 3d of June, and distinguished himself throughout that brilliant campaign, which culminated in the victories of Rich Mountain, Laurel Hill, and Carrick's Ford. At the battle of Rich Mountain, he rode fifteen feet ahead of his men; and though, as soon as the enemy discovered him, a shower of bullets were poured at him, it made no impression whatever on the coolness of the daring soldier. For "gallant and meritorious conduct" during that campaign, the President appointed him a Brigadier-General of Volunteers, on the 30th of July, 1861, and the appointment was confirmed four days later. When the health of General Kelly, who commanded at Romney, in Western Virginia, failed, he was assigned to that important command. The rebels under Jackson were within the jurisdiction, and he at once commenced operations with the view of driving them out. From various causes he was somewhat hindered in carrying out his programme, and when the rebels advanced on Romney, in January, 1862, he was compelled temporarily to retire.

These things, together with his failing health, induced him to tender his resignation to the President, but it was not accepted.

He then began work in earnest, drove the rebels from Romney and other positions, and on the 14th of February, 1862, announced in his official report that all the rebels had been driven out of his Department. It was on that day that the memorable charge at Blooming Gap took place. After an almost unprecedented march of forty-three miles in sixteen hours, over terrible roads, mostly at dead of night, they came upon the rebels at the Gap. Colonel Amstanzel was ordered to charge, but he disobeying, Lander charged on the enemy, followed by four others, put them to flight and captured seventeen commissioned officers. Conscious that he needed repose, after his brilliant victory, he asked to be relieved from duty; but, being refused, he did not press his request. True to his trust, he remained at his post to the last, and died like a soldier, with his harness on his back.

General Lander received his death-wound at Ball's Bluff, where so many of his comrades also met their fate. He was lying ill at Washington when he heard of the battle, but he left a sick-bed, rode forty miles, and arrived at the scene of action in time to render signal service. While conducting a reconnoissance, the day after the butchery of Colonel Baker, he received a painful wound in the leg. From the debilitating effects of this wound, aggravated, no doubt, by his herculean efforts to free his Department of the rebels, he died on the 2d of March, 1862, at Paw Paw, Virginia.

General Lander was a frank, bold, open-hearted man, of noble and generous nature, and commanding presence. He looked the soldier, every inch of him, and scorned to ask his men to go where he himself would not cheerfully lead the way. They knew this, and loved him as a brother. By his death, the country has lost one of its best men, and the tears of his command and the nation followed him to the grave.

BRIGADIER-GENERAL MICHAEL CORCORAN, U.S.V.

"O, Corcoran, thy fame be it mine to proclaim."

This brave and indomitable colonel, was born on the 21st of September, 1827, at Carrowkeel, county Sligo, Ireland. In 1849, he emigrated to America, and commenced business in New York; he also received an appointment in the post-office, and was clerk in the register's office just previous to his departure for the seat of war.

Colonel Corcoran began his military career in America by entering Company I (now Company A), of the Sixty-ninth, as a private, and by his soldierly qualities rapidly rose from the ranks, and was elected captain of his company. Captain Corcoran was elected colonel of the Sixty-ninth, August 25th, 1859. Since that time, his name and that of the regiment have been synonymous. On the visit of the Prince of Wales, Colonel Corcoran refused to parade the Irish-born citizens, in his command, to do honor to the son—however harmless—of the sovereign under whose rule those whom he believed to be the best men raised in Ireland for half a century were banished. His court-martial and defence are now matters of pride, not only among hundreds of thousands of his adopted fellow-citizens, but those who deem the subsequent conduct of England anything but a fair or grateful requital for the hospitality extended to her heir-apparent.

Upon the breaking out of this rebellion, its leaders built great hopes upon the Irish Democrats, and it is not too much to say, that Corcoran's upright and unselfish course at this juncture, was one of the most severe blows the sympathizers with secession at the North could have received. Many of the officers of the Sixty-ninth were doubtful of the propriety of "turning out" while their colonel was undergoing a court-martial for an act which they completely justified. Immediately Colonel Corcoran, in a public letter, implored them not to take him into any account, but to stand by the flag of the Union and the sacred principles involved in its sustainment. The court-martial was quashed; the Union sentiment of the Irish rushed like a torrent into the ranks of the army; and the Sixty-ninth left for the seat of war, attended by one of the most enthusiastic multitudes ever chronicled in our city history.

In the progress of the arduous labors assigned to his command, Colonel Corcoran won the esteem of the heads of the war department. From the time of its departure from New York until the battle of Bull Run, the Sixty-ninth won enduring honors, and the indomitable colonel gave his regiment unceasing examples of courage and patriotism. He greatly distinguished himself at Bull Run, and is the only one officially chronicled as having brought his regiment off the field in a hollow square. He was wounded, however, and falling into the hands of the enemy, he was carried to

Richmond; subsequently sent to Castle Pinckney, Charleston harbor; and in anticipation of an assault on the city of Charleston by the Port Royal expedition, was removed to Columbia, in the interior of the State. On the 26th of February, he was brought back to Richmond; but the traitors finding Richmond in danger, again hurried him off; this time to Salisbury, North Carolina.

Upon Colonel Corcoran, probably more than on any other of the Union prisoners, has public attention been fixed and public sentiment aroused. His conduct as a prisoner has reflected credit upon the Union soldiery, and the treatment he has received from the rebels has appealed deeply to the hearts of the whole community. The announcement that he was chosen as one of the hostages for the safety of the privateers condemned to death as pirates, sent an indignant thrill of pity and shame throughout the North, and a commission, composed of Messrs. Barney, Daly, O'Gorman, and Savage, used every exertion to procure his release, but without effect. The rebel authorities made many agreements to exchange him, but broke them as soon as they were made.

In April, 1862, Colonel Corcoran was appointed one of the Harbor Masters of New York, by the Governor of the State. On the receipt of the news of his appointment, he wrote, "I am obliged, under existing circumstances, respectfully to decline the acceptance of the appointment. Many reasons clearly demonstrate the propriety of my action, among which I mention the following: FIRST—If in the possession of my liberty before the termination of this wicked Rebellion, I desire to serve my country in the field, by assisting to suppress it; and, SECOND—I cannot possibly think of accepting a salary for duty really performed by another person. You will, therefore, please have any money which may have been paid to Mrs. Corcoran by Mr. Barber, immediately refunded; and as I have no opportunity at present of writing to Governor Morgan and expressing my sentiments, will you do me the favor of performing the service, and take occasion to express my warmest thanks."

Comment on the above is needless; the pure, unselfish character of the man shines through it all.

On the 13th of August, 1862, Colonel Corcoran was exchanged for General Buckner. His tour to New York was a journey of repeated triumphal receptions and ovations. In honor of his services and noble conduct while a prisoner, the President promoted him to the rank of brigadier-general in the volunteer service of the United States, and dated his commission, July 21st, 1861, the date of the battle of Bull Run.

On the 16th of October, General Corcoran was nominated as the Union candidate for Congress, from the fifth congressional district of New York, in opposition to Fernando Wood, the opposition candidate; but the General again declined civil office, preferring to serve his country in the field.

BRIGADIER-GENERAL LOUIS BLENKER, U.S.V.

> "He stopped the fliers;
> And by his rare example, made the coward
> Turn Terror into Sport; as waves before
> A vessel under sail, so men obey'd,
> And fell below his stern."

Louis Blenker was born in the city of Worms, grand-duchy of Hesse-Darmstadt, in the year 1812. His father was a jeweller, and the son was instructed in the same art, duly "served his time," and on arriving at the age of manhood, found himself a journeyman jeweller, with the world before him. Just then a large share of the attention of Europe was turned toward Greece. The three great European powers agreed in May, 1832, upon the election of Prince Frederick Otho, of Bavaria, as king of Greece, and Greece acquiesced in the choice. With the prince was to go a Bavarian legion of three thousand five hundred men, and immediately the drum went around for recruits. Louis Blenker was just then free from an apprenticeship served in a dull German city, and an adventurous life must have seemed to him possessed of every charm that fancy could give it; so he became one of the thirty-five hundred.

Otho, accompanied by the legion, embarked at Brindisi, January 24th, 1833, and landed at Napoli, on the 6th of February. Against Colocotroni, the Maïnotes and Roumeliotes, the Bavarian legion was employed in various directions, and in its ranks young Blenker saw four years of hard and almost incessant service. From a private he became a sergeant, and upon the disbandment of the corps, in 1837, he received the honorary rank of lieutenant. Thus honored, and elevated in the social scale, he returned to his home in Worms. From Worms he went to Munich, where he attended medical lectures, with a view to the adoption of that profession—either to kill or cure, he evidently thought his destiny. But his intention toward a profession was soon relinquished in favor of commerce, and he returned again to Worms, was married, and became established in the wine trade: such was his position when the troubles of 1848 began.

He became commander of the national guard in Worms, and upon the actual outbreak of the revolution, he took an energetic part in it. He joined the revolutionary army with a considerable force, and on May 10th, defeated a corps of the Baden army. Seven days after he occupied Worms, marched against Landau, and defeated at Boblenheim an equal force of Prussians. He then reëntered Baden and took command of the forces to sustain Mieroslawski. After the battle of Durlach, he occupied Muhlbourg and Knielingen. Driven from these posts, though not without a severe struggle, he lost his last opportunity in the revolution through his failure to seize Baden-Baden, by the possession of which he could have covered the disastrous retreat of the revolutionists. Upon the departure of Mieroslawski, he joined the forces of Sigel, his successor. But the popular movement was effectually crushed, and he retired into Switzerland. Thoughout his irregular struggle the forces under Blenker's command had behaved remarkably—and that more was not done with them, was the fault of their leader, who exhibited no conspicuous quality of soldiership, if we except the one of cool and resolute courage.

Blenker was ordered to leave Switzerland in September, 1849, and, embarking at Havre, he landed at New York, and soon after purchased a small farm in Rockland county. His farm not proving prosperous, he abandoned it for more active business in New York, in which he continued until the rebellion broke out. Raising a regiment—the Eighth New York Volunteers—he left New York with it on the 27th of May, 1861, for Washington, where it arrived the next day, and was quartered in various parts of the city until June 9th, when it went into camp on Meridian Hill. Shortly before the advance to Centreville, the Eighth New York was ordered into Virginia, and Colonel Blenker placed in command of the first brigade of the fifth division.

Upon the day when the battle of Bull Run was fought, the fifth division was in reserve, and Blenker's command formed upon the heights east of Centreville. Here it remained until the retreat of the United States forces began, when it advanced on the road to Warrenton, to protect the retreat and prevent an advance of the enemy. "Stretching far across the road, long before the hoped for refuge of Centreville was reached, was a firm, unswerving line of men, to whom the sight of the thousands who dashed by them was only a wonder or a scorn. This was the German rifle regiment; and to see the manly bearing of their general, and feel the inspiration which his presence gave at the moment, was like relief to those who perish in a desert." In this position Blenker held his men throughout the evening, and spread a sure protection over the multitude who fled disordered through his columns. At midnight the order to retreat was received, and the brigade moved on to Washington, which it reached in safety nineteen hours after. For these services, Colonel Blenker was commissioned a brigadier-general of volunteers, August 9th, 1861, and soon after was put in command of the fifth division of the Army of the Potomac.

BRIGADIER-GENERAL JAMES S. WADSWORTH, U.S.V.

> "For his Bounty,
> It had no Winter in't; an Autumn 'twas
> That grew the more by reaping."

JAMES S. WADSWORTH was born in Geneseo, New York, October 30th, 1807. He is the oldest son of James Wadsworth, Esq., one of the pioneers of Western New York. He received a thorough education at Harvard and Yale Colleges, from which he graduated with distinguished honors. He studied law with Messrs. McKown & Denniston, of Albany, New York, and completed his legal course in the office, and under the eye of the great statesman of New England, Daniel Webster, of Massachusetts. He was admitted to the bar in 1833, but has never practised, having been absorbed in the charge of his immense estates. In 1834, he married a daughter of John Wharton of Philadelphia.

His whole life has been mainly devoted to his private business. Although active and influential in moulding the politics of the country, and never neutral or silent upon any of the great questions before the people, he has rarely held office. His position, talents, wealth and liberality, all conspired to give him unusual prominence, and he has often been invited by the people and those in authority to accept high and honorable official positions, but he rarely consented. It was not until the necessities of the country demanded it, that he accepted office; and when she required him, he volunteered to serve in any capacity he could be made useful.

His public record, the leading points of which we take from the New York Era, may be briefly stated. He was presidential (Fremont) elector at large in 1856, and district (Lincoln) elector in 1860. He was appointed by the legislature of the State of New York, a Commissioner to the Peace Convention held at Washington, in February, 1861. In May, 1861, the Governor of the State of New York, offered him the appointment of major-general of the State volunteer force, which he declined. In August, 1861, he accepted from the President the appointment of brigadier-general of volunteers. On the 15th of March, 1862, he was appointed military governor of the District of Columbia. On the 24th day of September, 1862, he was unanimously nominated by a convention of the unconditional Union men of the State, called without distinction of party, for the office of Governor of the State of New York.

When the first gale of secession swept from the South, cutting off Washington from the North, leaving us all in doubt and uncertainty as to the fate of our capital, he, upon his own motion, at his own risk and expense, chartered two ships, freighted them with provisions, and started with them himself to Annapolis, Md., to provide for the State militia who were being hastened forward to defend the capital. It proved most timely, and met a want the Government was unable to supply. Having the confidence of the administration, and being the personal friend of General Scott, from that time to the battle of Bull Run he was employed in executing delicate and important military and civil commissions. He also took into the field his two sons, to share with him the fortunes of the war, and was also accompanied by his son-in-law. He did not desire that they or himself should survive the downfall of the Government.

When the army started upon its march to Richmond, he volunteered upon the staff of General McDowell, who had command of the army. In the memorable battle of Bull Run, he distinguished himself by his activity, coolness, courage and humanity, and received the commendations of General McDowell in his report of the battle, and the plaudits of the whole country.

General McDowell says : " Major Wadsworth stayed at Fairfax Court House late in the morning, after the retreat of the Union army, to see that the stragglers and weary and worn-out soldiers were not left behind. He spent the whole of the night after the battle in bringing up the rear with the soldiers who had been abandoned by their own officers, saving the government property, and ministering to the wants of the wounded." General McDowell in awarding credit to the members of his staff upon that day, says of General Wadsworth : "The latter, who does me the honor to be on my personal staff, had a horse shot from under him in the thickest of the fight."

He is a very liberal man, but always modest in the distribution of charities, preferring that no publicity be given to them. In all the great calamities which have befallen the people in different sections of the country, by fire and famine and disaster, he has always been a very large contributor. When Ireland was suffering from famine, he loaded a ship with food at his own expense and sent it over to the sufferers. He mingles freely with his friends and neighbors at home, and is held in high estimation and positive affection by them. He is the embodiment and representative of that irrepressible sentiment which pervades the loyal masses, and finds expression in the memorable words of Jackson : "The Union must and shall be preserved." The hopes of the people, and the liberal spirits the whole world over, beat high and strong for the salvation of the nation. Every pulsation of his heart, and every emotion of his soul is in unison with them.

BRIGADIER-GENERAL E. L. VIELÉ, U.S.V.

"The times need action! Round the soldier's name
In stormy periods gathers triple fame."

EGBERT L. VIELÉ was born in Waterford, Saratoga county, New York, on the 17th day of June, 1828. His family were among the first settlers in the State. On his father's side, Huguenots, who escaped from France into Holland at the time of their religious persecution, and came out to this country with the early Dutch settlers. On his mother's side he was descended from the famous Dutch family, Knickerbocker. His ancestors on both sides were holders of honorable office in the colonies, and defended their country, both in the wars against the Indians and the Revolution. His father was the Honorable John L. Vielé, judge of the Court of Appeals, and a member of the New York Senate.

Egbert received his early education at the Albany Academy, under the venerable Doctor Beck. In 1844, at the age of sixteen, he entered the West Point Military Academy, and graduated there with Generals Burnside and Griffin of the Federal army, and Heath and A. P. Hill of the rebel army, in June, 1847. He received the brevet of second-lieutenant in the second regiment of infantry, and was immediately ordered to Mexico, where he was assigned to duty with the first dragoons. As adjutant of the squadron, he was engaged in clearing the national road from Vera Cruz to Mexico of the numerous guerilla bands that infested it. At the close of the Mexican War he was promoted to the rank of first-lieutenant, and stationed for five years on the Texan frontier, in command of a battalion of dragoons. At the age of twenty-one he was honorably mentioned for gallantry in the discharge of his duties in the perilous war with the Camanche Indians.

In December, 1852, Lieutenant Vielé sent in his resignation, which was accepted, and, settling in the city of New York, became a civil engineer. For some time he held the office of State Topographical Engineer of New Jersey; and in 1856, under the direction of a board of commissioners, of which Washington Irving was president, preliminary surveys of the New York Central Park were made under his superintendence, and the commissioners adopted, for the laying out of the park, a plan presented by him, choosing him as the engineer-in-chief. Mr. Vielé was also consulted on all the great works in and about the city and harbor of New York. He was chosen chairman of the Sanitary Association, and vice-president of the New York State Geographical Society, and acted in these capacities with great credit.

When the great Southern rebellion broke out, Mr. Vielé occupied the position of

BRIGADIER-GENERAL E. L. VIELE, U. S. V.

captain of the engineer corps of the Seventh Regiment New York State Militia, which he had accepted two years previous. On the 28th of April, 1861, Captain Viélé arrived at Washington with one hundred and seventy-five recruits for the "Seventh," on the steamer "Daylight," making the first passage up the Potomac. The "Daylight" had but one howitzer, and came alone, under the very guns of the enemy's batteries. The President and Secretary of War met them at the navy yard, and the "Seventh" passed a vote of thanks for his brave passage.

On the 17th of August, 1861, the President appointed Captain Viélé a brigadier-general in the volunteer service of the United States; and on the 26th, the Government opened a camp of instruction at Scarsdale, Westchester county, New York, under his command. A better drill-master and disciplinarian there is not; and all regiments under him are subjected to the most thorough discipline.

On the 21st of October, Flag Officer Du Pont's expedition left Annapolis for Port Royal with General Sherman on board, with a large land force. General Viélé commanded the first brigade, about six thousand men, thus being the second in command. After disembarking on the 13th of November, and remaining a few weeks at Hilton Head, he made an advance up the Savannah River, and was engaged in throwing up those wonderful pieces of engineering on that river, and Tybee Island, which resulted in the investment and reduction of Fort Pulaski on the 11th of April, 1862.

This having been accomplished, General Viélé returned to New York on a short furlough, and went to Washington to ask for more active duty in the field, and accompanied the President and Secretary of War to Fortress Monroe. While there, an attack on Norfolk, Virginia, was planned, and to General Viélé was assigned the duty of leading the advance. On the 10th of May, he landed at Ocean View, and on the afternoon of the same day the city surrendered, and General Wool appointed General Viélé its military governor. He still holds this position, maintaining, by his dignified courtesies to the conquered, and his unflinching determination, that makes no compromise with a rebel against the Government he represents, the respect of both enemies and friends.

In 1850 he was married to Miss Teresa Griffin, daughter of the late Francis Griffin of New York city.

General Viélé is the author of "Reports on Central Park Improvements," "Sanitary Laws," "Mining Reports," "Engineering Reports," "Viélé's Hand-book of Active Service, for the use of Volunteers," etc., etc. All these, together with his high literary tastes, entitle him to the position of a polished scholar as well as a successful soldier and wise administrator.

BRIGADIER-GENERAL JAMES SHIELDS, U.S.V.

"And he smote them hip and thigh, with great slaughter."

JAMES SHIELDS is a native of Tyrone county, Ireland, where he was born in the year 1810. He first came to this country in the year 1826. In 1832, he went West, and settled in Kaskaskia, one of the oldest villages of Illinois, where he devoted his energies to the study and practice of the law. He was soon after elected to the State Legislature, and in 1839 was made State Auditor. Four years later he was appointed Judge of the Supreme Court, and in 1845, having received from President Polk the appointment of Commissioner of the General Land Office, he removed to Washington. Upon the breaking out of the Mexican War during the following year, Mr. Shields was appointed a brigadier-general of United States Volunteers. His commission was dated July 1, 1846.

He was present at the siege of Vera Cruz, and was particularly noted for his gallant conduct. At the battle of Cerro Gordo, he greatly distinguished himself, and freely shed his blood in defence of his adopted country's honor.

A recital of General Shield's deeds at that battle seems more like the details of the great actions of some famed hero of romance than the plain narrative of the conduct of "one of Polk's raw generals," as the opposition styled him when appointed. Severely wounded, he continued on the field, urging on his men, until a ball, passing through his lungs, struck him down. He was carried from the battle-field, and was reported so near dead that obituary notices appeared of the gallant general in nearly all the papers of the country. Even in the neighborhood of the battle ground his life was for weeks despaired of, and the anecdote of his cure is remarkable, as it would appear improbable did the man not live among us at the present time to verify the statement. It appears that he was entirely given over by the army surgeons, when a Mexican doctor said he would live if he would let him remove the coagulated blood from the wound. Shields, as a kill or cure remedy, told him to try, and a fine silk handkerchief was worked and finally drawn through the wound, removing the extravasated blood, when daylight could be seen through the hole. And to-day General Shields is a hale and hearty man, free from disease or any inconvenience from a wound which, at the time of its infliction, was pronounced mortal, having been made by a large copper ball and going directly through his body and lungs.

For his gallant and meritorious conduct on this occasion he was in August, 1848, breveted a major-general of volunteers. Still suffering from his wounds, we find him commanding a brigade in the valley of Mexico, consisting of a battalion of marines and regiments composed of New York and South Carolina volunteers. He was also in the battle of Chapultepec, where, being unhorsed, he fought on foot, bareheaded and in his shirt sleeves, leading his brigade, sword in hand, with a bravery that has made his name remarkable in American history. He was again dangerously wounded; but his vigorous constitution enabled him to rally from the effects of his injury, and he recovered. The brigade he commanded, after performing valorous deeds, ending in the capture of the city of Mexico, was disbanded on the 20th of July, 1848. The war being ended, General Shields laid down the sword, and assumed once more his place in civil life.

On his return to the State of Illinois, he was elected United States Senator from that State. Owing to some technicality, he was refused admission as a Senator, when he promptly resigned the post and was as promptly reëlected. He returned to Washington, and for six years proved himself to be as able in council as he was on the battle-field. In 1855, he left the Senate, leaving at the same time Illinois, and went to settle on the lands awarded to him for his services in the army, which lands he had selected in the Territory of Minnesota. When that tract became a State, General Shields was returned to represent it in Congress as a Senator, and took his seat after its admission in May, 1858. General Shields having drawn the short term, he had to vacate his seat in 1859, and not securing a reëlection, he went further west into California. From his retirement he was again brought out by the great rebellion, having been appointed by Congress a brigadier-general, with a commission dating from August 19, 1861. This commission he at first refused; but, deeming it his duty to stand by his adopted country in her troubles, he came forth, and, after a long voyage, reached Washington, D. C., where (his name, in consequence of his refusal, having been stricken from the army list) he waited some time before he obtained a command. The death of General Lander left that division without a head, and General Shields was at once appointed to the command, with the rank of brigadier-general, his division forming part of the corps d'armée of General Banks.

General Shields is of good personal appearance, about five feet eight inches in stature, with dark hair and complexion. His style of speaking is easy, fluent and agreeable; a progressive Democrat; but, at the same time, a strong supporter of the Government of the United States in its unity and integrity.

BRIGADIER-GENERAL A. DURYÉE, U.S.V.

"But there are deeds which should not pass away,
And names that must not wither."

ABRAM DURYÉE, a soldier worthy of his noble Huguenot descent, was born in the city of New York, on the 29th of April, 1815, and was educated at the Grammar School of Columbia College, after graduating at the Crosby street High School. Concluding his studies, he commenced business as a mahogany merchant, in which pursuit he has succeeded in making a large fortune.

General Duryée commenced his military career as a private in the One Hundred and Forty-second Regiment N. Y. S. M., Colonel Graham, and served as general guide, quartermaster and sergeant-major. In 1838 he entered the ranks of the Seventh Regiment, N. G., passed through all the grades of non-commissioned officers with distinction, and became a second-lieutenant in 1840. He was rapidly promoted through all the higher grades, and on the 29th of January, 1847, succeeded to the colonelcy of the famous Seventh Regiment. During the eleven years of his command, Colonel Duryée, by his industry and military and executive ability, won for his regiment a world-wide reputation for efficiency, discipline and moral bearing, unequalled by any other regiment in the nation.

With Duryée at its head, the "gallant Seventh" has quelled every riot in the city of New York, including the bloody riots at the Astor Place Opera House, at the City Hall, in the sixth ward, the "Dead Rabbits," etc. He also commanded the regiment at camps Trumbull and Worth at New Haven and Kingston; at Newport; on excursions to Boston to attend the celebrations of the Bunker Hill and Warren monuments; and to Richmond with the remains of President Monroe, visiting on their return Mount Vernon, Washington and Baltimore. On the 4th of July, 1859, Colonel Duryée resigned his commission; and though the regiment waited upon him in a body, earnestly soliciting him to remain with them, it was in vain. He retired to private life, the recipient of compliments and testimonials, such as no other officer has received.

When the slaveholders of the South struck the paricidal blow at the life of the nation, Colonel Duryée resolved to enter the field, and commenced to organize, discipline and drill the Fifth Regiment N. Y. S. V., better known, however, as "Duryée's Zouaves." So great was his reputation as an able and gallant leader, that the ranks were quickly filled, and the regiment was one of the first in the field. After one month's instruction at Fort Schuyler, the regiment embarked on board the steamship

BRIGADIER-GENERAL A. DURYÉE, U.S.V.

"Alabama," on the 23d of May, 1861, and on their arrival at Fortress Monroe, two days later, encamped near the Hampton Bridge. On the 27th, Colonel Duryée was placed in command of Camp Hamilton as acting brigadier-general. On the arrival of General Pierce, Duryée returned to his regiment. On the night of the 9th of June, 1861, he received orders to march on Little and Great Bethel. He reached Great Bethel in the morning, and though the enemy were defended by masked batteries of great strength, he made many attempts to charge them with great bravery; but, being prevented by the creek, withdrew to the rear by command of General Pierce, and took up his return march. On the retirement of General Pierce, Colonel Duryée was again placed in command as acting brigadier-general; but, after the defeat at Bull Run, most of the brigade were ordered to Washington under Colonel Baker, and Colonel Duryée again returned to his regiment. They were soon after ordered to Baltimore, and encamped at Federal Hill, where they constructed a formidable and extensive fort.

On the 31st of August, 1861, the President appointed Colonel Duryée a brigadier-general in the volunteer service of the United States, and placed him in command of one of the largest brigades in the service, near Baltimore.

In compliance with his oft-repeated request, he was at length sent to the front, in command of a brigade in General McDowell's corps d'armée. After Jackson's raid in the valley of the Shenandoah, Duryée formed a junction with Ord at Thoroughfare Gap, on the 11th of June, 1862, and took Front Royal. Returning to Culpepper, he received orders to join Banks at Slaughter Mountain, where he arrived in the evening and fought gallantly by moonlight for six hours till midnight. Then, falling back from the Rapidan to Haymarket, constantly giving battle to the enemy, he was ordered to Thoroughfare Gap to intercept Longstreet. They reached the Gap on the 28th of August, and fought the enemy till dark. Being overpowered by superior numbers, he fell back and joined the army on the old battle-field of Bull Run, August 29th. The next morning he advanced into the woods, driving the enemy before him; but, during the heavy fire of the enemy, General Duryée was wounded in the foot, but gallantly remained at his post. At Chantilly, he held the advance of Hooker's division. They were then ordered into Maryland.

Passing through Frederick City, they arrived at South Mountain in time to reinforce Meade's division. Though exhausted by a twelve hours' march, his brigade ascended the almost inaccessible mountain amid redoubled cheers, and gallantly repulsed the enemy and drove them to the bloody field of Antietam. Here, this heroic brigade, reduced to one hundred men, held the deadly cornfield against overwhelming numbers and a terrific fire. Its leader was constantly in the front and escaped by miracle, having two horses shot under him, and all his staff either wounded or dismounted. New York is justly proud of her gallant soldier.

BRIGADIER-GENERAL T. F. MEAGHER, U.S.V

> "In the morning beam
> Gay trumpets sound, and gorgeous banners stream;
> The charger's hoof, impatient for the start,
> Beats time responsive to the rider's heart.
> On to the battle! With one cheerful cry
> A thousand voices swear to do or die."

THOMAS FRANCIS MEAGHER was born on the 3d of August, 1823, in Waterford, Ireland. He was educated by the Jesuit Fathers, from 1834 to 1843, at Clongowes Wood, in the county Kildare, Ireland, and at Stoneyhurst, Lancashire, England. At both these famous colleges he gave early promise of the splendid oratorical powers by which he has since been so remarkably distinguished.

Leaving Stoneyhurst in 1843, he soon, even while preparing for admission to the Irish bar, became known and recognized in the political world as a leader, especially amongst the party called "Young Irelanders," who, contrary to the teachings and wishes of O'Connell, inculcated a resort to physical force as the only practical means of securing Irish independence. This, just then, in Ireland, was daringly patriotic and perilous; for, in 1846 and 1847, the desolating famine which prevailed, prematurely urged on revolutionary projects. In vain did Meagher and his brother-chiefs heroically take the field and call for followers. The poor famine-stricken people, being unarmed and powerless, after an insignificant struggle, Meagher, with O'Brien, McManus, and O'Donohoe, were arrested, tried for, and found guilty of, high treason to England's queen, and sentenced to be hanged, drawn, and quartered; a sentence subsequently commuted to transportation for life to Van Dieman's Land.

From thence, early in 1852, he escaped, and arriving in the latter end of May in New York, was received with boundless enthusiasm by all classes. On the 7th of June he was presented with a congratulatory address by the City Corporation, in which he was tendered a public reception, and the cause he personified sympathized with. The sympathies he graciously accepted; the public reception and its proposed festivities, he respectfully declined. Since then he has been eminently distinguished as a popular lecturer, brilliant writer, explorer of Central America, and member of the New York bar, to which he was admitted in September, 1855.

On the breaking out of the great Southern rebellion in 1861, he at once proclaimed for the Union, and raising a dashing band of young Irishmen, over one hundred strong, equipped them as Zouaves and led them to Virginia, where, at his desire, they were attached to Colonel Corcoran's Sixty-ninth New York State Militia, as company K. Captain Meagher was beloved and esteemed by the whole regiment, as a most promising officer, and one to be unfalteringly followed. Acting as major at the fierce battle of Bull Run, he justified this confidence by his firmness in skillfully holding the men under fire and leading them to the charge.

Immediately on the return of the three months' volunteers, Captain Meagher projected and commenced, with the authority of the War Department, the organization of the Irish Brigade. In this he was assisted by most of the gallant officers of the Sixty-ninth N. Y. S. M.; who, having served with him in the old organization, proudly accepted him as their leader in the new. Toward the latter end of November, the brigade, consisting of the sixty-ninth, eighty-eighth, and sixty-third regiments New York State volunteers, with two batteries of artillery, after being presented, from the residence of Archbishop Hughes, by the ladies of New York, with appropriate and elegant flags of green and gold, left for Virginia.

His commission as brigadier-general, bearing date February 3d, 1861, was unanimously ratified by the United States Senate, and amid the greatest enthusiasm, he immediately took command. On any arduous march, or throughout the twenty-one days of constant skirmishing on the Peninsula, before McClellan commenced moving from the Chickahominy to the James River, during which the regiments of the Irish Brigade were the sole reliance in Sumner's command for picket duty, as they have subsequently been its unconquerable reserves; or on any of the battle-fields on which they fought and bled, General Meagher was never absent from his command. At Fair Oaks, where the sixty-ninth and eighty-eighth, with other portions of Sumner's corps, hurled back the enemy who had overwhelmed Casey's and Couch's divisions: at Gaines' Mills, where the brigade, with that of General French, when disastrous rout seemed inevitable, rushed to the front and stemmed the fury which had borne back Fitz John Porter's gallant corps: at Peach Orchard, at Savage's Station, at White Oak Swamps, at Charles City Roads, at Malvern Hill, where, while the three regiments in the frenzy of battle, like the sweep of an eagle, dashed into the fray, Fitz John Porter, kindling into rapture, cried out to their general, "I envy you the command of that brigade!"—in each and all of these battles, in which Irish valor was preëminent, General Meagher was its inspiration as well as leader. And so, too, it was at Antietam, where the brigade, under a murderous fire, unsupported, splendidly carried a steep hill occupied by the enemy in force, and defended from behind natural breastworks. General Meagher's horse was here shot under him, and, in consequence of his fall, he himself severely bruised.

The gallantry of the Irish Brigade has been repeatedly publicly acknowledged. At Harrison's Landing, General McClellan thanked it for its "superb conduct in the field;" and after Antietam, General Sumner hailed it as "bravest of the brave!" General Meagher is proud of his "noble little brigade," as may also, of him and it, be every lover of the Union which they sprang to arms to save.

BRIGADIER-GENERAL WILLIAM H. L. WALLACE, U.S.V.

> "Nothing in his life
> Became him like the leaving it. He died,
> As one that had been studied in his Death,
> To throw away the dearest thing he own'd,
> As 't were a careless trifle."

WILLIAM HENRY LAMB WALLACE was born in Urbana, Ohio, on the 8th of July, 1821. His parents were in moderate circumstances, intelligent and highly respected. His father was a man of mark, in his sphere, for quick intelligence and sound judgment.

In the year 1834, young Wallace went with his father's family to Lasalle county, Illinois, and in 1839, to Mount Morris, Ogle county, Illinois, where the family resided till the death of the father. Up to this time, William's opportunities for education were very limited. At the Rock River Seminary, opened in Mount Morris, in 1841, he received instruction in the common and higher English branches; and so rapid was his advancement that in 1844, he was employed as a teacher in that institution.

In 1845 he commenced the study of law with Judge Dickey, at Ottawa, Illinois; and here his success was such that for years previous to his death he ranked with the first lawyers of the state.

When the call was made for soldiers to carry on the Mexican war, Wallace was among the first to volunteer. He enlisted as a private, carrying a musket, in Company I, First Regiment Illinois Volunteers, led by the lamented Hardin. His merits there successively won for him the position of Sergeant, Lieutenant, and Adjutant. He was Colonel Hardin's Aid, and stood close beside that gallant leader when he fell on the field of Buena Vista.

At the close of the Mexican war he returned to his office at Ottawa, and devoted himself to his profession, which rapidly brought him wealth and renown. As one of the fruits of his industry, may be seen a stately mansion, surrounded by most beautiful grounds, in the northern suburbs of Ottawa, Illinois, where, with his accomplished lady, the eldest daughter of Judge Dickey, he was long accustomed to bestow kindly and large-hearted hospitality upon an extensive circle of friends and acquaintances.

At the commencement of the Great Rebellion, Wallace enlisted with the Eleventh Illinois Volunteers, was chosen colonel of that regiment, and immediately took the field. For months he was Acting Brigadier and commandant at Bird's Point.

BRIGADIER-GENERAL WILLIAM H. L. WALLACE, U.S.V.

At the siege and bloody battles of Fort Donelson, Colonel Wallace led the second brigade of General McClernand's division. Leaving Fort Henry on the 11th of February, he arrived before Donelson on the morning of the 13th, when the battle opened with the artillery, and a cannonading was kept up all day. At noon, the brigade charged bravely on the enemy's middle redoubt, marching gallantly up the hill to the very foot of the works; but in the perfect *feu d'enfer* that came from the enemy's guns, they were withdrawn by General McClernand. The night was one of great hardship; but their spirits never flagged, notwithstanding they were without tents or fire, exposed to the wind and driving snow-storm, and assailed by the enemy's shot. The 14th passed in comparative quiet, but on the morning of the 15th, the battle continued with redoubled vigor. Colonel Wallace's brigade again advanced to the brow of the hill, and, with the courage of veterans, compelled the enemy to fall back. They gave place, however, to another line of fresh troops, who were also compelled to give way. But his men were falling fast from the terrible fire of the enemy's batteries on his front and both flanks, and Colonel Wallace fell back half a mile. Having procured a supply of ammunition, he returned again to the assault, this time driving him within his intrenchments. The next morning, the 16th, the enemy surrendered, and Colonel Wallace hoisted the Stars and Stripes over the conquered Fort. For his bravery and signal services in this battle, he was promoted to the rank of Brigadier-General in the Volunteer service of the United States, on the 3d of March.

On the bloody field of Shiloh, General Wallace commanded Major General Smith's division, on the extreme left of the whole army. At ten o'clock on the morning of Sunday, the 6th of April, the battle opened; and until four in the afternoon, General Wallace's division manfully bore up. Their musketry fire was absolutely continuous; and the artillery was admirably served, with but little intermission through the entire time. Four times the rebels charged on them, and each time they were repulsed with heavy slaughter. But now, every division but Wallace's had fallen back; to remain in isolated advance would be madness. Just as the necessity for retreating had become apparent, General Wallace, whose cool, collected bravery had commanded the admiration of all, fell, mortally wounded. At last the division fell back, bearing the body of their beloved leader, and black night soon closed around this great climax to the bloody tragedy of this Sabbath day! The blood of Wallace, with that of Ellsworth, Lyon, and Winthrop, calls aloud to Heaven for vengeance! vengeance on the heads of the authors of this infamous rebellion, that has made them martyrs in the holy cause of Freedom!

BRIGADIER-GENERAL C. GROVER, U.S.V.

> "Such are the hearts we want, for where such are,
> Freedom and peace, glory, security,
> Never desert the land."

CUVIER GROVER was born on the 29th of August, 1828, in Bethel, Maine. Entering the West Point Military Academy at the age of eighteen, he graduated fourth in the class of 1850, receiving on the 1st of July the commission of a second-lieutenant in the Fourth United States Artillery, in which regiment he served until 1853, when he was detailed on topographical duty with the Northern Pacific Railroad survey under Governor Stevens. In January, 1854, he, with four Canadian voyageurs and a dog train, explored that portion of the contemplated railroad route from the head-waters of the Missouri to Fort Wallah Wallah. In this region, hitherto unexplored in winter, the cold was so intense as to freeze the mercury in the thermometer and the dogs in their tracks. For Lieutenant Grover's valuable services in the expedition he was promoted to a first-lieutenancy in the tenth infantry.

In 1857 he accompanied Colonel A. S. Johnson's expedition against the Mormons of Utah, was provost marshal, and in the following year was promoted to a captaincy. In the spring of 1860, when most of the troops were recalled from Utah, Captain Grover was transferred to New Mexico, where he served until the breaking out of the great rebellion in 1861.

In the latter part of that year, Captain Grover obtained a leave of absence to serve in the volunteer force, and on the 14th of April, 1862, was appointed a brigadier-general of volunteers, and assigned to the command of a brigade in Hooker's division of the army of the Potomac. He joined his command before Yorktown, and, upon its evacuation by the enemy, led the advance of Hooker's division. Early on the morning of the 5th of May, 1862, he attacked the enemy's rear-guard near Williamsburg, and sustained the conflict with his brigade until the arrival, about nine o'clock, of the rest of Hooker's division. For twelve hours our advance was under a heavy cross fire of artillery, carried the enemy's works, and slept on its arms where night overtook it. At Fair Oaks, also, General Grover greatly distinguished himself.

When General McClellan made his retreat from the Chickahominy to Harrison's Landing, General Grover had his share of toil, danger, and privation during the famous "seven days." On the 29th of June, during the retreat, his brigade was placed in position on the right of General Hooker's division, which supported General Sumner's left in repulsing the enemy's attack near Savage's Station. On the following day it was again brought into action, and rendered signal service in repulsing the enemy, who, having forced back General McCall's division, attempted to cut in two our retreating army near Glendale. On the following days of the retreat, General Grover's brigade occupied other important positions, and did good service in the cause. On the arrival of the army of the Potomac at Harrison's Landing, on the James, to him was assigned the duty of holding the key to its defences. While here, his command formed part of an expedition which made a reconnoissance in force to Malvern Hill, and upon the evacuation of Harrison's Landing, marched to Yorktown as part of the rear-guard.

When Hooker joined Pope, Grover, of course, accompanied him, and took an active and enviable part in the battles of Bristow Station and Bull Run the second. They reached the old battle-field of Manassas at an early hour on the morning of the first day's fight. The action had already commenced from right to left. The division was not in the immediate conflict, however, until afternoon, when it became necessary to break the enemy's centre if possible. With this view, General Hooker ordered General Grover, about three o'clock P. M., to advance and dislodge the enemy from his strong position behind a railroad embankment, and to occupy and hold the woods beyond. Being aware that the enemy were in great force, and protected by a most formidable breastwork, General Grover advanced in line of battle, after having instructed his command to move slowly until it felt the enemy's fire, then rapidly until at close quarters, fire one round, and rely on the bayonet for the rest. The order was executed admirably; and then occurred one of the most desperate bayonet charges, and, for a short time, one of the bloodiest contests of the war. At the embankment our lines were checked, and a hand-to-hand contest ensued, with bayonets, knives, and pistols, and the lines were marked by rows and piles of dead. The check, however, was of short duration; and, led on by their brave general, who had two horses shot under him, the gallant brigade rolled back the enemy's first line from the embankment, then the second and more compact line behind it, and finally, with thinned ranks, dashed upon the third. Being entirely unsupported, a further advance was impossible; the line wavered, and they were finally forced to retire with a loss of more than a quarter. After this great battle, General Hooker's division was so reduced as to make it necessary to rest and reorganize, General Grover's brigade alone having lost on the field about eleven hundred out of about thirty-five hundred.

On the 6th of December, 1862, a powerful armada left New York, freighted with an immense army, commanded by that most noble leader Major-General Banks. The second division was led by General Grover. What wonder then, with such chieftains, that success should wait upon their footseps?

BRIGADIER-GENERAL MAX WEBER, U.S.V.

"Strike home, and the world shall revere us
As heroes descended from heroes."

MAX WEBER, son of Dr. Ludwig Weber, was born at Achern, in Baden, on the 27th of August, 1824. He was educated at the military academy of Carlsruhe, in the Grand Duchy of Baden, where he graduated in 1842, and entered the ducal service with a second-lieutenant's commission. In 1844 he was promoted to the rank of adjutant, and in 1848 served with considerable distinction in Schleswig-Holstein in the campaign against the Danes.

In the next year the great revolution broke out, and Weber was given the command of a brigade, Sigel's advance guard. He participated in numerous skirmishes and battles, and shared all the dangers with his gallant men. To recount in detail his career in Germany would be to repeat that of his noble leader, Franz Sigel. Weinheim, Grossachsen, Waghausel, Sinsheim, Rastadt, and Kuppendeim saw his prowess and his ability as a leader. The disastrous result of Germany's struggle for liberty is well known. Colonel Weber, with his brave compatriots, Sigel, Willich, Schurz, Hecker, Blenker, and thousands of participants, were exiled, and came to this country in 1850.

When the breaking out of this gigantic rebellion against the lawful authority of the United States, for the purpose of spreading the curse of slavery over this fair land, brought the people of the loyal North to their feet in amazement and indignation, her adopted citizens, who had once fought, and bled, and suffered in the holy cause of freedom, were by no means slow to again do righteous battle in its defence. The Turnverein resolved to form itself into a rifle regiment, and by a unanimous vote tendered its command to Colonel Weber, who at once accepted it. On the 6th of May, 1861, he received his commission as colonel of the Twentieth Regiment of New York State Volunteers, or United Turner Rifles. The regiment was soon filled, and on the 13th of June, after the presentation of several banners and patriotic speeches at the City Hall, they embarked for Fortress Monroe, where they were stationed at Camp Hamilton.

On the 14th of August, Colonel Weber set sail with General Butler's expedition, on Flag-Officer Stringham's squadron, for Cape Hatteras. They landed on the 28th, and in the afternoon made an assault on Fort Clark and captured it; and on the next morning advanced on Fort Hatteras, which soon surrendered to General Butler. General Butler, in his official report, says: "While all have done well, I desire to speak in terms of especial commendation, in addition to those before mentioned, of the steadiness and cool courage of Colonel Max Weber, who we were obliged to leave in command of a detachment of three hundred men on a strange coast, without camp equipage or possibility of aid, in the face of an enemy six hundred strong, on a dark and stormy night."

After the surrender of the forts, Colonel Weber was put in command of them, and remained there until the 12th of September, when he returned to Fortress Monroe and was placed in command of Camp Hamilton. While here, nothing occurred to break the monotony of the daily routine of camp life, saving the defeat of the rebels in a skirmish at Newmarket Bridge, December 22d, 1861, and the ever-memorable conflict between the "Monitor" and "Merrimac."

On the 28th of April, 1862, Colonel Max Weber was promoted to the rank of brigadier-general in the volunteer service of the United States.

On the morning of the 11th of May, 1862, General Weber landed at Ocean View with six regiments, accompanied by Generals Wool and Vielé, the President, and Secretaries of War and the Treasury. He proceeded at once against Turner's Creek Bridge, held by the rebels with three pieces of artillery, which opened a brisk fire at his approach. They soon fell back, however, after firing the bridge, which compelled General Weber to make a forced march of five hours before reaching the intrenchments, which he found evacuated. They reached Norfolk without further hindrance, and were met at the suburbs by the Mayor and Common Council, who surrendered the city. The capture of Norfolk effected also the destruction of the iron-clad steamer "Merrimac" by the rebels, to prevent its falling into our hands.

After a short stay at Norfolk, General Weber was put in command at Suffolk, where he remained until the 11th of September, when he was ordered to join General McClellan at Boonesborough, Maryland, which he did with characteristic promptness and energy, arriving there on the 16th. He was at once detailed with his brigade to French's division of Sumner's corps.

The next morning, Weber, in the advance, engaged the enemy, at first driving him back by a gallant bayonet charge. They being rapidly reinforced, in turn pressed Weber's troops to their first position, which they held under a heavy fire of musketry and artillery, which made many gaps in their lines. General Weber, seeing the great importance of his position, led on his troops again and again, through four hours' hard fighting, until his brigade was relieved. Just before being relieved, he was struck by a musket ball in his right forearm, shattering the radius. An exsection of the bone was performed with difficulty, and he is now very slowly but surely recovering.

Since General Weber's entrance into the service of the Union, he has received, through the influence of his father, full amnesty and invitation to return to his native land; but, a citizen of this country, he does not wish to leave it until it is restored and saved for the great principles of liberty and humanity.

BRIGADIER-GENERAL JOSEPH B. CARR, U.S.V.

*"We thank the gods,
Our Rome hath such a soldier!"*

JOSEPH BRADFORD CARR was born in the city of Albany, New York, on the 16th of August, 1828. He is one of ten children of William and Ann Carr, natives of the Emerald Isle, who came to this country in 1824. Joseph's father was by trade a mason, and extraordinary efforts must have been put forth to provide necessary comforts for such a large family. Besides, the facilities for acquiring even an elementary education were fewer and less available at that time than they now are; consequently our young hero was cut off from the advantages accruing to an early education.

From these few lines, which can only touch the leading points of a life pregnant with interest, and marked with many salient points of singularly felicitous events, it will readily be seen that fortune, promotion, and position in the world, whether in civil or military life, may be secured from the humble walks of life. Poverty is no barrier to genius. This was especially true of him whose history is now before us. When a boy, love of home, filial affection, dutiful regard to parental authority, endeared him to the family circle. These were the tender fibres which were bound around his youthful heart, and in his manhood form those strong ligaments which develop not only the soldier and the hero, but the patriot and citizen.

In the year 1849 the Republican Guards was organized in Troy. He at once offered himself as a candidate, and was accepted. He remained a private for one year, when he was promoted to a sergeantship. Soon after he was elected to the position of second-lieutenant, and again to that of first-lieutenant. Then followed Lieutenant Carr's promotion to a captaincy, in which position he served for four years. His military genius and aptness to teach prepared him for further distinctions. In 1858 he was elected major of the Twenty-fourth Regiment of New York State Militia; and on the 10th of July, 1859, he was chosen its colonel, which important position he held with honor to himself and great satisfaction to the regiment.

On the breaking out of this gigantic rebellion—at this crisis of our history, when the nation lived months in a single hour—Colonel Carr was one of the first to offer his services to sustain the nation in all its integrity. In company with Major G. L. Willard, he raised a regiment, the Second New York Volunteers, in Troy and its vicinity, which speedily reached the maximum required by the Government. It was found that Major Willard could not be detached from the regular army, and,

BRIGADIER-GENERAL JOSEPH B. CARR, U. S. V.

with singular unanimity. Colonel Carr was elected as the commander of the regiment, May 10th, 1861. On the 18th, the regiment left Troy for the seat of war, one thousand strong. Embarking at New York, on board the steamer "James Adger," on the 22d of May, they arrived at Fortress Monroe two days later, were they disembarked, and went into camp at Newport News.

On the night of June 9th, General Pierce left Fortress Monroe to attack Great Bethel, and Colonels Allen and Carr were ordered to hold their commands in readiness to move. Early on the morning of the 10th occurred the unfortunate mistake of Colonel Bendix, and Allen and Carr were sent on. Arriving at Great Bethel, Colonel Carr was placed on the left, supporting Greble's battery, where they fought bravely, and never turned back until General Pierce gave the order to retreat.

On the 11th of June, 1862, Colonel Carr was placed in command of the third brigade of Hooker's division as acting brigadier-general. In this capacity he served with honor at Fair Oaks, Glen Dale, and Malvern Hill, and displayed his prowess at every point. He was the "ever-present man." To recount his many gallant deeds in the bloody and disastrous campaign of the Peninsula would be to repeat those of his brave commanders, Heintzelman and Hooker. In the midst of the raging battles, when bullets were flying thick and fast, he was reminded of his danger; but, dauntless and courageous, he moved along in front of his battalions, securing the confidence of his soldiers, and receiving repeated plaudits from the commanders around him.

When Hooker joined Pope at Bull Run, on the 26th of August, Colonel Carr accompanied him, and in the ensuing terrible battle won new honors and greener laurels. Nor did he go unrewarded. "For gallant and meritorious conduct in the field," Colonel Carr was promoted to the rank of brigadier-general of volunteers on the 7th of September, 1862.

But General Carr's services did not end here. South Mountain and Antietam saw his prowess, and their bloody fields testify to his glory. Bravely he fought, as indeed he has ever fought; and wherever he trod, victory followed in his footsteps.

Few men have secured a wider fame, or won a greater reputation in so short a time, than Colonel Carr. The secret is, it has been earned. A single incident in proof of this sweeping statement may be named. During the entire campaign, he has not been absent from the tented field for a single day or night. Always at his post, watching with a vigilant eye every movement, no wonder he has received repeated and flattering notices from his superiors.

BRIGADIER-GENERAL J. H. HOBART WARD, U.S.V.

"Ab uno, disce omnes."

John Henry Hobart Ward was born in the city of New York, in the year 1823.

Colonel Ward volunteered his services to his country for the Mexican War, in the year 1847, and served under General Taylor in all the engagements from Corpus Christi to Monterey, and under General Scott from Vera Cruz to the city of Mexico.

On his return from Mexico, General Lee, then commissary general of the State of New York, after repeated efforts, succeeded in obtaining his services as assistant. The system introduced in that department, and the faithful manner in which he discharged his duty, secured him the appointment of commissary general, as successor to General Lee, which office he held for two succeeding terms.

An extract from a letter by General Scott, dated December 10th, 1856, will be read with interest. He says, "General Ward served with me in the campaign between Vera Cruz and the capital of Mexico, with great zeal, activity and distinction, and has always cherished the character of a good soldier, good citizen and gentleman."

When the great rebellion broke out in 1861, he commenced the raising of a volunteer regiment in the city of New York for the war. His character as an officer and a brave man, soon secured him the requisite number of men, and he was mustered into the service of the United States on the 3d of June, and crossed with his regiment into Virginia on the 7th of July.

At the battle of Bull Run, on the 21st of July, 1861, he was mentioned in all official reports with great praise. An extract from a letter by General Kearney, dated Fair Oaks, June 9th, 1862, says, "Colonel Ward was distinguished at Bull Run;" and in another letter from the same lamented general, he says: "Colonel Ward was greatly distinguished in Mexico. In this rebellion, he has fulfilled those noble antecedents. At Bull Run, in 1861 his State had no occasion to blush for him, nor the thirty-eighth regiment."

An extract from General Hooker's report of the Battle of Fair Oaks, says: "The second brigade was not yet up, and apprehensive that the troops engaged might be overcome, all of my staff officers were dispatched to find and press it forward; as there was delay, orders were given Colonel Ward to support my command, which were promptly responded to by that gallant officer, and his brigade was brought into action on the right of the New Jersey regiments. . . . . . My warmest thanks are also tendered to Colonel Ward for the promptness with which his brigade was brought into action, and the gallant manner in which he fought it."

BRIGADIER GENERAL J. H. HOBART WARD, U.S.V.

Colonel Ward was with his regiment in General Kearney's division again at the battle of Williamsburg, on the 5th of May, 1862, of which in a letter he says: "At Williamsburg, my report testified to Colonel Ward's noble bearing and peculiar gift of influencing men to follow to victory." General Kearney's official report of this great battle says: "I ordered Colonel Ward, with the Thirthy-eighth Regiment N. Y. V. (2d Scott Life Guard), to charge down the road and take the rifle pits (in the centre of the abattis) by the flank. This duty Colonel Ward performed with great gallantry—his martial demeanor imparting all confidence in the attack."

Colonel Ward was again with his regiment on the 31st of May, and on June 1st was in command of the brigade of which General Kearney in a letter said: "Colonel Ward has again rendered conspicuous service, and was in command of the brigade (Birney's) on the 1st inst., when it achieved a great victory."

Colonel Ward was with his regiment in the battles at Warrenton and Bull Run; and at Chantilly, on the 1st of September, 1862, he was again in command of the brigade, and the enemy were routed. The brigade is spoken of by all as having fought bravely on this occasion under his command, and as having again been victorious.

Colonel Ward has not only been conspicuous on the various occasions mentioned in the reports from which we have been allowed extracts, but has during the entire campaign of the Peninsula: at the siege of Yorktown, and the numerous skirmishes and exposures of that campaign, as well on the advance as at Savage's Station, Charles City Cross Roads, Malvern Hills, and Harrison's Landing, on the retreat from before Richmond, always in the heat of the engagements, and sustaining himself with heroic bravery.

Colonel Ward having been strongly recommended for appointment as brigadier-general of volunteers by the most distinguished officers of the army, and by all his superiors in command, on the exclusive ground of "meritorious conduct in the field," was appointed to that rank on the 4th of October, 1862.

The country may well be proud of the services of such a man; and could the present army have such commanders, the rebellion would soon be crushed out, and peace and tranquillity again restored to this once glorious nation.

COLONEL HENRY WILSON, 22D MASS. VOLS.

> "And thou shalt aye be honorably known
> As one who bravely used his tongue and pen
> As best befits a freeman,—even for those,
> To whom our law's unblushing front denies
> A right to plead against the life-long woes
> Which are the negro's glimpse of Freedom's skies."

HENRY WILSON was born in Farmington, New Hampshire, on the 16th of February, 1812. At the age of ten, he was apprenticed to a farmer in his native town, for whom he worked steadily for eleven years, during which period he attended the public school four weeks in each year, and read nearly a thousand volumes. On attaining his majority, Mr. Wilson apprenticed himself to a shoemaker in Natick. In two years he had accumulated money enough to enable him to attend the academies at Stafford and Wolfsborough, New Hampshire. He returned to Natick in 1838, and engaged in the shoe manufacturing business until 1848.

He took an active part in the presidential campaign of 1840, and made upward of sixty speeches in behalf of General Harrison. During the next eight years he was repeatedly elected to the House of Representatives, and was twice chosen a State Senator. He steadily voted for anti-slavery measures, and in 1845 introduced resolutions, which were adopted, against the extension of slavery, and made one of the fullest and most comprehensive speeches on the subject ever delivered. When the Whig National Convention, in 1848, refused to pledge the party to opposition to the extension of slavery, he renounced his connection with them, and became one of the founders and leaders of the Free-soil party. He purchased at this time the "Boston Republican," which he edited for two years, during which also he acted as chairman of the Massachusetts Free-soil State Committee.

In 1850 and 1851 he was president of the State Senate. In 1852 he was made president of the Free-soil National Convention at Pittsburg, and chairman for the next four years of the Free-soil National Committee. In the same year he was the Free-soil candidate for Congress, and in the following year for governor. In 1855 he was elected a United States Senator, and took an active part in organizing the Republican party. His first speech in the Senate was in favor of the repeal of the Fugitive Slave Law, and of the abolition of slavery in the Territories and in the District of Columbia. He has since taken part in all the important debates of the Senate, and has always spoken and voted on the side of freedom, and of free labor.

COLONEL HENRY WILSON, 22D MASS. VOLS.

His speech in March, 1859, in reply to Senator Hammond of South Carolina, who had stigmatized the laborers and mechanics of the North as "mudsills," attracted great attention. His prompt and bold defence of Northern rights several times involved him in personal difficulties with the arrogant upholders of slavery; and on the occasion of the outrage on Charles Sumner, he was challenged by Mr. Sumner's assailant, Preston S. Brooks, for denouncing the act as a "brutal, murderous, and cowardly assault." In a manly letter he declined to accept the challenge, on the ground that duelling is a barbarous practice, which the law of the land has stigmatized as a crime.

In January, 1859, he was reëlected to the Senate by an almost unanimous vote, and when it assembled in March, 1861, in extra session, he was made chairman of the committee on military affairs. The civil war made this a position of unprecedented labor and responsibility. Immediately on the outbreak of hostilities in April, he went to work with great vigor in aiding the preparations for the war, and in drafting military bills. He introduced the acts authorizing the employment of five hundred thousand volunteers; increasing the regular army; increasing the medical corps of the army; providing for the purchase of arms, ordnance and ordnance stores; for the better organization of the military establishment; for increasing the pay of privates, and various other nearly as important and patriotic measures. Some idea of the magnitude and value of his services may be formed from the fact, that General Scott said that Senator Wilson had done more work in the short extra session of 1861 than all the chairmen of the military committees had done for twenty years; while Secretary Cameron says, in a letter dated January 27, 1862: "No man, in my opinion, in the whole country, has done more to aid the War Department in preparing the mighty army now under arms."

After the adjournment of Congress, General McClellan invited him to join his staff, which he accordingly did for a brief period. But as the enlistment of volunteers began to slacken, he hurried home at the end of August, 1861, and issued a stirring appeal to the men of Massachusetts to rally around him for the defence of the country. In less than forty days he enlisted two thousand three hundred men, and organized the Twenty-second Massachusetts Regiment of Infantry, besides a company of sharpshooters, nine companies of the twenty-third regiment, and two batteries of artillery. He promptly led the twenty-second regiment, of which he had been appointed colonel, to Washington, together with the company of sharpshooters and a battery of artillery. He was placed in General Porter's division at Hall's Hill, but, at the urgent request of the Secretary of War, he resumed his position as aide on General McClellan's staff, which he held until January 9, 1862, when his senatorial duties called him from the field to the halls of the capital. In the session of 1862, most of the acts of Congress for the increase, efficiency, and comfort of the army were introduced by him, as was also the bill to abolish slavery and the slave code in the District of Columbia.

COLONEL RUSH C. HAWKINS, 9th N.Y.S.V.

> " I have marshall'd my clan,
> Their swords are a thousand, their bosoms are one!
> They are true to the last of their blood and their breath,
> And like reapers descend to the harvest of death!"

RUSH CHRISTOPHER HAWKINS was born on the 14th of December, 1831, in Pomfret, formerly a suburb of Woodstock, but now an independent town of Vermont. At eight years of age he became an orphan by the death of his father. For some time he was a cadet in the military school of Colonel Partridge, at Norwich, Vermont, and in his thirteenth year proceeded to Boston, whence he sailed on board the sloop-of-war "Plymouth," then commissioned as an escort to the Dead Sea expedition. After visiting the chief towns on the Mediterranean shore, he returned to the United States, and finding the country engaged in the Mexican War, he entered the second regiment of dragoons, and was in Mexico during the most exciting period of that war. At the end of the war he left the service and travelled for nearly two years in the South and West, seeing much of Southern life and manners. He then came to New York city, where he studied law, and entered into partnership with his cousin, Dexter A. Hawkins. In the summer of 1860 he married Ann Mary, the eldest daughter of the late Honorable Nicholas Brown, of Warwick, Rhode Island, who was, in 1844, consul-general at Rome, and afterwards lieutenant-governor of Rhode Island.

Mr. Hawkins was convinced that the slaveholders would soon rebel, and in the spring of 1860 he commenced the organization of a company formed on the Zouave drill. When President Lincoln called for seventy-five thousand volunteers to put down the rebellion, Mr. Hawkins, who had been unanimously chosen president of the Zouave company, at once offered their services to the State, and they were accepted, under the title of the Ninth New York Volunteers.

On the 5th of June, 1861, they were sent to Newport News, and arrived the day before the disaster of Big Bethel. Had General Pierce not given so hasty an order to retreat, the result would have been very different, as Colonel Hawkins was on his way to reinforce the national troops. While they were stationed at Newport News, General Butler appointed him president of the commission to try all military offenders.

In August, Colonel Hawkins participated in the Hatteras expedition, where his cool and collected bearing was conspicuous. On the return of Colonel Weber to Fortress Monroe, he was put in command of the forts at Hatteras as acting brigadier-general. On the 5th of October occurred the action at Chicamacomico, where he displayed his usual promptness and ability. The 15th of January, 1862, brought the Burnside expedition, and the 5th of February saw its departure from Hatteras with Hawkins and his gallant Zouaves on board. On the afternoon of the 7th, the troops landed on Roanoke Island, and the next morning proceeded to the attack, Colonel Hawkins leading the advance of General Parke's column. They soon passed the centre column, and charged bravely through the swamp, and up a narrow causeway swept by a thirty-two-pounder, in the face of a terrible fire of grape and musketry. As they neared the battery, General Reno emerged from the woods on the left, and the rebels fled in disorder. But a moment after, the Zouaves dashed over the ditch and up the side into the work, and then pursued the flying foe.

Much against his will, he was left at Roanoke Island when Burnside went to Newbern in March. But that wise leader had other work for him to do. On the night of the 19th of April, General Reno disembarked at Elizabeth City, and marched on Camden, with Colonel Hawkins in the advance, commanding the first brigade. Jaded as were his forces, on coming within range of the enemy's battery, eager for the fray, they bravely charged on it. "It was a most gallant charge," says General Reno in his report; "but they were exposed to a most deadly fire of grape and musketry, and were forced to retire, but rallied immediately." Another charge, however, compelled the enemy to retreat; but, our men were so fatigued by the intense heat and their long march that we could not pursue them. Colonel Hawkins displayed conspicuous courage. On their return, General Burnside issued a congratulatory order on their success and good conduct in the action.

Colonel Hawkins accompanied Burnside to the Peninsula and thence to the second battle of Bull Run and South Mountain, but his greenest laurels were won on the gory field of Antietam. On the afternoon of Wednesday, the 17th of September, Burnside made that famous charge across the stone bridge of Antietam creek. The bridge was swept by a rebel battery of six guns, but Hawkins and his Zouaves, "*Toujours prêt*," dashed forward, and, after an obstinate contest of several hours, carried the bridge, found the enemy ready drawn up under cover of the hills, and advanced in line of battle on the enemy's new position, half a mile distant. The enemy's guns kept up a terrible fire on our advancing line, which never wavered, but slowly toiled along. As they came up the hill they received a heavy volley from a large force of infantry behind a stone wall, about two hundred feet in front of the enemy's batteries. Our men, though terribly decimated, gave them a volley in return, and then went on with the bayonet. The enemy did not stay to contest the ground, and, although two to one, broke and ran; and the brave Zouaves, leaving two hundred and thirty-seven of their number on the field, were again covered with glory.

When Colonel Hawkins embarked at New York, the gentle breeze spread out the silken banner in the bright sunshine, and the golden words, "*Toujours prêt*," shone with unwonted brilliancy. How well he has redeemed the promise, Hatteras, Chicamacomico, Roanoke, Camden, Bull Run, South Mountain, and Antietam testify.

E. E. Ellsworth

COLONEL E. ELMER ELLSWORTH, 11th N. Y. S. V.

> "Columbia bends in sadness now,
>   Above her gallant soldier's grave;
> Laurel and cypress deck the brow
>   Of the dead Zouave—so young, so brave."

EPHRAIM ELMER ELLSWORTH was born at Malta, Saratoga county, New York, on the 11th of April, 1837. His father's fortunes were wrecked in the financial crisis of that year, he never was able to retrieve them, and Elmer was thrown on his own resources. Deprived of opportunities for advancement, after various employments in Troy and New York, and ineffectual efforts to enter West Point, for which the studies he had ardently pursued admirably fitted him, but from which the want of political patronage excluded him, he sought the West, and at Chicago, before he came to man's estate, was successfully engaged in business as a patent agent. Energetic and attentive to his affairs, he was soon building up his fortune; but, like many a noble-hearted man, beheld the fruit of his toil swept from under him by the fraud of one whom he had trusted. He then began the study of law, earning a livelihood at the same time by copying. Though he had thus chosen a profession, and devoted himself with his energy and intellect to acquire it, his ambition was to become a soldier. Himself a perfect gymnast, an accomplished swordsman, and a splendid marksman, he had a noble end in view. Our militia system was little better than a farce, composed mostly of "carpet knights," who hardly knew what a soldier was. Ellsworth's object was to turn these actors into soldiers, and his beau ideal of a true soldier was a Zouave. To this end, he devoted himself to a thorough study of the tactics. Having perfectly mastered it himself, he organized on the 4th of May, 1859, the United States Zouave Cadets of Chicago. He flung aside the relics of the old awkward dress, and adopted one that left the limbs and joints at liberty; but his régime was as strict as the garb was loose. Total abstinence from intoxicating liquors and tobacco, was a strict law, the violation of which blotted the name of the offender from the roll. At the United States Agricultural Fair, Ellsworth's Zouaves won the colors, and in turn held them as a prize to any company who could exhibit a similar efficiency. In July, 1860, they made a tour to the East, inviting any of the militia companies to compete with them for the colors. Their exercises were visited by crowds, and the New York Academy of Music was the scene of an exhibition which filled it as densely as the most popular singer ever did. On his return to Illinois he formed a volunteer regiment, which he tendered to the governor,

COLONEL E. ELMER ELLSWORTH, 11th N.Y.S.V.

as if conscious that war was inevitable. Ellsworth was now known and appreciated.

In the Presidential campaign, he was a warm supporter of Mr. Lincoln, and advanced his cause by eloquent and stirring speeches in various parts of the State. At the request of the President, Ellsworth accompanied him to Washington, and received a lieutenant's commission, as a preliminary to his entrance into the War Department, where he hoped to create the Militia Bureau, of which he had long been preparing the plan.

Disgusted with the chicanery and corruption of Washington, he threw up his commission and hastened to New York, to raise a regiment among the firemen of that city. A short interview with John Decker, the chief of the Fire Department, settled all to his satisfaction. That officer issued a requisition appealing to the department for volunteers. In two days, twelve hundred recruits had enrolled their names and proceeded to Fort Hamilton to drill. New York was enthusiastic over her Fire Zouaves, and three stands of colors were presented to them. The first was presented by the Fire Department, and the second by the Hon. John A. Dix, on behalf of Mrs. Astor. Then, escorted by five thousand of their fellow firemen, the regiment marched first to the Astor House, where Mr. Stetson presented them with a third stand of colors, in the name of the ladies of the house; then to the Baltic, where they embarked for Washington, which they entered on the 2d of May, amid an ovation equalling that which had attended their departure from New York.

On the 22d of May, orders were given to commence the march into Virginia the following morning. Accordingly, at two o'clock, A.M., Ellsworth and his Zouaves crossed in steamboats to Alexandria, but on their arrival found that the town had already surrendered. Satisfied that no resistance would be offered, Colonel Ellsworth gave orders to interrupt railroad communication, and proceeded himself with a small party to seize the telegraph. On his way thither, he caught sight of the rebel flag floating from the Marshall House. The gallant colonel and his party immediately ran up to the roof, cut down the flag, hoisted the stars and stripes, and were descending the stairs when Jackson, the proprietor, sprang forward from a corner, and aimed a fowling-piece at Ellsworth's breast. Private Brownell endeavored to strike up the weapon; but the assassin's grasp was firm, and a slug entered Ellsworth side, driving into his very heart a gold circlet with the legend: "Non nobis, sed pro patria."

His murderer died almost as soon. Brownell, failing to thrust aside the piece, drew back and sent his rifle-ball through the forehead of Jackson, and with a single impulse, thrust him through. They raised their beloved colonel and laid him on a bed; but life was extinct. He now sleeps quietly on the hill-top, near the place of his birth, with the flag for which he died so nobly floating over him; but his spirit walks abroad. "Remember Ellsworth," is the soldier's war-cry. Aye! he will always be remembered; and when this rebellion and its infamous authors shall sink into oblivion, the name of ELLSWORTH shall ever be associated with all that is noble, patriotic and self-sacrificing!

COLONEL JAMES A. MULLIGAN, MO. VOLS.

> "The fight had ceased! The cannon's roar
> Was silent on Missouri's shore;
> The leader and his band so brave
> Had turned from walls they could not save."

JAMES A. MULLIGAN was born in Utica, New York, in the year 1829. His parents were natives of Ireland. His mother, after the death of his father, which took place when he was a child, removed to Chicago, Illinois, where she has resided with her son since 1836.

James was educated at the Catholic College of North Chicago, under the superintendence of the Rev. Mr. Kinsellar. He is a strict member of the Catholic Church.

In 1852, 1853, and 1854, he read law in the office of the Hon. Isaac N. Arnold, congressman from the Chicago district. For a short time he edited the "Western Tablet," a semi-religious weekly paper, in Chicago.

In 1856, he was admitted an attorney-at-law. At this time he held the position of second lieutenant in the Chicago "Shield's Guards," one of the companies afterwards attached to the Irish Brigade.

In the winter of 1857, Senator Fitch, of Indiana, tendered him a clerkship in the Department of the Interior. He accepted the position, and spent the winter in Washington. During his residence there, he corresponded with the "Utica Telegraph," over the *nom de plume* of "Satan."

After his return from Washington, he was elected captain of the Shield's Guards. On the news arriving of the bombardment of Fort Sumter, he threw his soul into the national cause. The Irish-American companies held a meeting, of which he was chairman. Shortly afterward he went to Washington with a letter written by the late Senator Douglas, on his death-bed, to the President, tendering the service of a regiment, to be called the "Irish Brigade." He was elected colonel, and immediately went to work with a will. The course of the Brigade up to the battle of Lexington, is well-known; it has nobly, bravely and honorably done its duty.

On the 16th of September, 1861, General Price surrounded Colonel Mulligan, at Lexington, and made an assault on the works, but was repulsed, after a hard day's fight. The rebels procured bales of hemp, rolled them in advance, and under their cover, succeeded in securing a position in the rear. They made but few assaults, their object being to cut off supplies of water, which was done on the morning of the 18th. Human endurance could not stand it much longer, and, at length, on the 20th of September, after a fifty-nine hours' severe and horrible fight, without water, in which the gallant Colonel was severely wounded, he reluctantly, and with tears, surrendered his emaciated little band of two thousand men, to Price's overwhelming army of thirty-five thousand, as prisoners of war. Such an heroic defence has hardly its equal upon the pages of History, and the name of MULLIGAN will stand high among the defenders of their country.

Refusing to give his parole, the indomitable Colonel was hurried off with Price's retreating army, accompanied by his heroic wife, who determined to sacrifice all to share his captivity. He was at length exchanged on the 1st of November; and on the 20th of December, Congress passed a resolution thanking him for his gallant defence of Lexington, and authorizing the 23d Regiment of Illinois Volunteers to inscribe on their colors, the name "LEXINGTON," in letters of gold.

Colonel Mulligan is worthy of all praise. A purer, better man does not live in the state of Illinois. Since he was able to tell the difference between ale and water, a glass of spirituous or malt liquor has not passed his lips. He is a rigid temperance man, although he is jocund, and whole-souled to a fault. He is six feet three inches in height, with a wiry, elastic frame, a large, lustrous hazel eye, an open, frank, Celtic face, stamped with a courage, pluck and independence, surmounted with a bushy profusion of hair, tinctured with gray. He is a fine scholar, a good speaker, a brilliant writer, and a promising lawyer.

Honorable in all relations—respected by all—he has won his way upward by untiring industry and unquestionable courage.

MAJOR THEODORE WINTHROP, U.S.V.

"March we must, ever wearily,
March we will; true men will be true."

THEODORE WINTHROP was born in New Haven, Connecticut, September 21st, 1828, and was a lineal descendant of the first John Winthrop, who in 1630 led out from England one of the noblest of the many Puritan colonies, and became himself governor of the commonwealth of Massachusetts. His father was Francis Bayard Winthrop, a gentleman of wealth and education. His mother is a grand-daughter of President Dwight, and a sister of President Wolsey. Thus Winthrop's very name is pervaded with New England virtues and memories. He entered Yale College from the well-known school of Messrs. French, of New Haven, and graduated with the class of 1848, covered with honors.

Soon after graduation, Winthrop, and others, formed the first class in the "School of Philosophy and Arts;" a department established the year previous, and opening before the youthful scholar a broader range of studies worthy of his best ambition. Severe mental work, added to private literary studies, proved too much for his frame. His physicians told him he must travel. Giving up the plans of theology, literature and law, which he had successfully formed in choosing a profession, he embarked in July, 1849, for Europe. By his journal, we find him arriving at London, August 28th; in Paris, November 23d; and at Rome, January 9th. With eyes, ears, and pen continually busy, he spends February in traversing eastern Italy, March in Greece, April in northern Italy, and, after tramping in a sturdy pedestrian tour through Germany and Switzerland, returns to Paris in September.

In April, 1851, three months after his return, Mr. Winthrop entered the Pacific Mail Steamship Company, at the invitation of W. H. Aspinwall, Esq., whose acquaintance he had made in Europe. In September, he recrossed the Atlantic, to place Mr. Aspinwall's son and nephew at school in Switzerland, and, after revisiting some of the more interesting portions of Germany, enters upon his old duties in January, 1852. The ensuing autumn finds him in Panama, in the employment of the steamship company, and almost well and happy. The tropics, where physical life is most intense, varied and perfect, is a new world. Everything invites and promises adventure. The spirit of travel is strong upon him, and he cannot be quiet. Nature speaks, and he is her child, and must ever listen with reverence and joy to her many voices. After often traversing the Isthmus with the treasure-parties, he returned home by way of San Francisco.

MAJOR THEODORE WINTHROP, U. S. V.

He returns to the counting-room in November; but his heart and fancy are still abroad. Accordingly, in January, 1854, with Mr. Aspinwall's consent, he joins Lieutenant Strain's expedition to prospect for a ship-canal among the Sierras of the Isthmus, and would have perished from hardships had he not wandered from his party and been forced to make his way back to the ship. Returning to New York, he began in March the study of law in the office of Charles Tracy; and after his admission to the bar, in 1855, remained with him as clerk another year.

The following summer finds him travelling in Maine with Church the artist, and under their mutual inspiration he drinks in nature with the soul of a poet and the eye of a painter. He returned to enter the political campaign of 1856. Long since a Republican in heart and by scholarship, he canvassed extensively for Fremont in Pennsylvania. After the issue, he established himself in law at St. Louis; but the climate and life not suiting, he returned in July, 1858, to find at last his true calling—the field of literature and authorship.

But, at the fall of Sumter, Winthrop dropped the pen and grasped the sword. The acts which followed all know. He joined the Seventh regiment at New York; marched with it to Washington, sharing its hardships and its fatigues; became, at Fortress Monroe, a member of General Butler's staff, as aide and military secretary, with the rank of major; and aided in planning the attack on the batteries of Great Bethel, where, on the disastrous 10th of June, 1861, he fell in the van, his firm, wiry form erect, waving his sword, and calling his comrades on into the very jaws of death.

"On the 19th of April, 1861, he left the armory-door of the Seventh, with his hand upon a howitzer; on the 21st of June his body lay upon the same howitzer at the same door, wrapped in the flag for which he gladly died as the symbol of human freedom. And so, drawn by the hands of young men lately strangers to him, but of whose bravery and loyalty he had been the laureate, and who fitly mourned him who had honored them, with long, pealing dirges and muffled drums, he moved forward."

In a quiet *escritoire* were found, undreaming of publication, a little pile of manuscripts, Winthrop's golden legacy to an admiring, yea, an almost worshipping people. Of these, "Cecil Dreeme," "John Brent," "Edwin Brothertoft," "The Canoe and the Saddle," "Isthmiana," "Life in the Open Air," "The March of the Seventh New York to Washington," and "Love and Skates," are already published—but a small portion of the novels, tales, essays, and poems which shine among his papers. There is no dullness in them: every page sparkles with light and life; the people talk in epigrams; he comes ever near the face and heart of his great teacher, Nature. The brave, noble author wrote freely as a man of the world, yet purely as a woman, never letting fall a word unworthy of his high-toned mind and virtuous soul.

Though he has left us, he is not dead. The brave, like the good, die never. He lives—destined to be an inspiring historic name of this great war against oppression.

CAPTAIN THOMAS R. HAINES, 1st N. J. CAV.

"O! it is great for our country to die, where ranks are contending;
Bright is the wreath of our fame; glory awaits us for aye—
Glory that never is dim, shining on with light never ending—
Glory that never shall fade, never, O! never, away!"

THOMAS RYERSON HAINES, son of the Honorable Daniel Haines, formerly Governor of New Jersey, and now a Justice of the Supreme Court of that State, was born at Hamburgh, in the county of Sussex, March 15th, 1838. Having graduated at the College of New Jersey in 1857, and read law for the requisite term, a part of which was spent at the Law School of the University of Cambridge, he was admitted to the bar of New Jersey in June, 1860, and commenced practice at the city of Newark.

In politics he adopted the principles avowed by the Democratic party; but secession he denounced as a political heresy; the storming of Fort Sumter, as an overt act of treason; and the armed rebellion which followed, as an assault upon the life of the nation, to be repelled and suppressed by all the nation's force. From the time of that insult to the American flag, he was resolved to offer his services to his country. In August, 1861, he was commissioned first-lieutenant of company K, First New Jersey Cavalry. Accustomed to the saddle from childhood, and dexterous in the use of the broadsword, that arm of the service pleased him most; and within ten days of the notice of his appointment, he took leave of home and the loved ones there, and reported himself for duty at Trenton.

Early in September the regiment moved to the vicinity of Washington city. Then the task of drilling raw recruits was commenced in earnest, and accomplished with success; his rule being, "never to undertake to drill the men in any movement without first thoroughly understanding it himself." While exacting strict obedience to every order, he scrupulously sought to promote the personal comfort of his men, attending carefully to their supplies, and watching over them in sickness and in health. Nor was he indifferent to their moral training. He persuaded his company to listen daily to a portion of Scripture. The reading of the orderly not being satisfactory to all, Lieutenant Haines assumed the exercise himself, reading selected passages, explaining, and sometimes commenting upon the text. His labors were not confined to the duties of a lieutenant. He was called to the office of regimental judge advocate, for which his legal attainments well qualified him. On the urgent solicitation of the commander, he assumed the duties of the adjutant of the regiment. Afterwards he was commissioned as captain of company M. In every capacity he took a full share of all the hardships and perils encountered by the regiment, which, from the time it was brigaded, was almost constantly made the advanced or rear guard.

On the 25th of May, 1862, the brigade, under General Bayard, was moving from Fredericksburgh toward Richmond, when it received orders to join the forces of General Fremont in pursuit of the rebel general, Jackson. By forced marches, it reached Strasburgh on the evening of Sunday, June 1st. The next morning, the First New Jersey Cavalry charged through the village, and upon the rear of Jackson's retreating forces. A succession of skirmishes ensued, and the batteries of the enemy, placed at commanding points to cover his retreat, were charged or flanked, always with success, but not without loss.

On Friday, June 6th, having driven the enemy through Harrisonburgh, Colonel Wyndham, in command, in making a reconnoissance beyond the town, fell into an ambuscade, and was, with others, captured, and a number of his officers and men killed and wounded. In the engagement they met, hand to hand, the celebrated regiment of Ashby's cavalry, and a terrific conflict ensued. Captain Haines encountered the renowned Colonel Ashby himself, and during the contest, Ashby fell—by whose hand there can be no positive assurance, but some who were present ascribe it to that of the subject of this memoir. When the retreat was sounded, Captain Haines, continuing in the rear of his company, found himself pursued by three rebel horsemen in advance of others. He wheeled toward them with sabre drawn, and endeavored to rally his men. The rebels checked their horses, but his call was not heeded, perhaps not heard. Being unsupported, he was compelled to retire, and while wheeling, he received a ball from the pistol of the most advanced of the horsemen, and he fell to rise no more. This horseman was the noted Major Green. A rebel trooper, as if in revenge for the loss of his leader, dashed up to Captain Haines, as he lay prostrate and almost lifeless, and inflicted a sabre cut on the head. One who was present says of him: "Never was greater heroism displayed. Surrounded on all sides, he yet fought with the courage of an ancient Spartan, and twice he cut his way through; but a pistol ball in his right side unhorsed him, and after he had fallen, all the remaining pulsations of his warm heart were ended by a ghastly sabre cut."

The next day, officers in search of the body, found it near the battle-field in a newly-made grave, prepared by a good Dunker. Having no coffin, he lined the bottom and sides of the grave with green branches; then, spreading a cloth over the face and placing a board over all, he filled it with earth; thus saving from further mutilation the fair features and graceful form of a young officer and doing a kindly act to the remains of one whom he had never known in life. It was enough for this Christian philanthropist that he had once been his fellow-being.

On Sunday, the 8th of June, the body was re-interred in the cemetery at Harrisonburgh, Va., with all the honors due to a colonel, voluntarily rendered by the whole regiment, every officer and man appearing like a chief mourner.

Such was the short and brilliant career of a gallant soldier and a true man. None was more beloved, few could be more lamented.

CAPTAIN JOHN FOOT, 2D MINN. VOL.

"His earthly record is, that he lived an unblemished life, and died virtually and really a voluntary sacrifice to the noble cause of Constitutional Freedom and Order."

JOHN FOOT, the son of Samuel Alfred and Jane Campbell Foot, was born on the 30th of April, 1835, in the city of New York. In the spring of 1847 his parents removed from the city to the village of Geneva, N. Y.

After suitable preliminary preparation, he entered Williams' College in September, 1851, and graduated in July, 1855. In September of that year, he went to the city of New York, and commenced the study of law in the office of William E. Curtis, Esq., and was admitted to the Bar in December, 1856. He pursued his profession till October, 1860, when impaired health obliged him to seek a more propitious climate in the West. He left the city for the prairies of the West, in accordance with eminent medical advice. Here he very rapidly regained his health, or seemed to do so, and arranged to commence anew the practice of the law, with flattering prospects of prosperity and success. With that view, he went to Red Wing, in Minnesota, and on the 15th of April, 1861, was admitted "as an attorney and counsellor to practice in all the courts" of the State of Minnesota.

But, now a new career is suddenly opened before him, the standard of Rebellion had been lifted up in the land. The call of the government sounded out, summoning to its aid the spontaneous support of patriot volunteers, and thousands were flocking to uphold the imperilled interests of public order, and to vindicate the time-honored but insulted flag of the Union. Captain Foot deemed it his duty to aid in this patriotic work. He soon raised a company, and was commissioned by Governor Ramsay on the 31st of July, 1861, as captain of Company I, in the Second Regiment of Minnesota Volunteers. That regiment, after being thoroughly drilled for several months, entered into active service in Kentucky in October, 1861. It went through an active winter's campaign in that State. The series of brilliant successes that crowned the arms of the Union in that section of the country, began with the battle of Mill Spring, on the 19th of January, 1862. The regiment to which young Foot belonged bore a most gallant and conspicuous part. Colonel McCook, acting brigadier, in his report states, that the Second Minnesota were within ten feet of the enemy, and at first the contest was almost hand-to-hand—the enemy and the Second Minnesota were poking their guns through the same fence at each other! There are very few instances on record in which officers and soldiers have shown an equal amount of bravery. The rebels could not stand before it.

CAPTAIN JOHN FOOT, 2d MINN. VOL.

But, in the meantime, the personal and private experience of Captain Foot discloses a sad but most heroic record, that remains to be briefly told.

The humidity of the climate, the exposure of the camp, and the toils of the march, began to show their effects, and it very soon became apparent that his health was likely to be totally undermined. But how could he retire from the service at this most critical juncture? How could prudential considerations be listened to when the enemy was just at hand? Every thought of self, every considerate regard to health, had to give way to the point of honor and the impulse of patriotism. Think of the quiet and uncomplaining heroism that could still go forward in such circumstances as these! Think of the weary and protracted march, the broken rest, the unavoidable and perpetual exposure to wind and weather, with an enfeebled constitution! Think of the excitement and tumult of the battle that ensued, and of the word of military command still continuing to issue firmly and steadily from attenuated lips, and from a breast already weakened and wasted by the ravages of disease! It was not until all these things were gone through, and the army returned, successful and victorious to the camp, that our youthful soldier felt himself at liberty to turn his attention to himself.

On the 29th of January, 1862, Captain Foot returned to Minnesota, under instructions to recruit his regiment. He repaired to his post of duty, but his health rapidly declining, and being no longer able to serve his country, he was unwilling to be a burden to it, and on the 24th of February offered his resignation, and betook himself to the home and refuge of his early childhood. He arrived there on the 1st of March, and expired on the 13th, aged 26 years. His remains were interred at Geneva, on Sunday afternoon, the 17th of March, 1862.

REV. A. B. FULLER, CHAPLAIN 16TH MASS. VOL.

"Be soldiers of the country if need be, in her present urgent perils; but above all, be Soldiers of the Cross."

ARTHUR BUCKMINSTER FULLER was born August 10, 1822. He was early instructed by his father and his sister, Margaret Fuller. At the age of twelve, he spent one year at the Leicester Academy. In August, 1839, he entered Harvard University, at the age of seventeen, and graduated in 1843. During his college course he united with the church connected with the University. Immediately on graduation, he purchased Belvidere Academy, in Belvidere, Boone county, Illinois, which, assisted by a competent corps of instructors, he taught for the two subsequent years. During this time, Mr. Fuller occasionally preached as a missionary, in Belvidere and destitute places. He was a member of the Illinois Conference of Christian and Unitarian ministers, and by them licensed to preach. His first sermon was preached October, 1843, in Chicago. In 1845, Mr. Fuller returned to New England; entered, one year in advance, the Cambridge Theological School, and graduated in August, 1847. After preaching three months at West Newton, to a society of which Honorable Horace Mann was a principal founder and a constant attendant, Mr. Fuller accepted a call to the Unitarian Society in Manchester, New Hampshire, and was subsequently ordained March 29th, 1848. In September, 1852, Mr. Fuller received a call from the New North Church, on Hanover street, in Boston, one of the most ancient churches in the city, being founded in 1714, and a church built that year on the spot where the present one now stands. This call Rev. Mr. Fuller refused, the relation between himself and the Manchester Society being a most happy one. The call was, however, renewed and ultimately accepted, and Mr. Fuller was installed in Boston, June 1, 1853.

In January, 1854, Mr. Fuller was chosen by the Massachusetts House of Representatives, chaplain of that body. In 1858, he was elected by the Massachusetts Senate their chaplain, both of which appointments he accepted and discharged their duties. In the same year he was chosen by the State Temperance Convention a member of the Executive Committee, and was elected a director of the Washingtonian Home, better known as the Home for the Fallen.

Mr. Fuller's published writings are, "A Discourse in vindication of Unitarianism from popular charges against it," Manchester, 1848. "Sabbath School Manual of Christian Doctrines and Institutions," Boston, 1850. "A Discourse occasioned by the death of Hon. Richard Hazen Ayer, delivered in the Unitarian Church, February 18, 1853." "An Historical Discourse, delivered in the New North Church, October 1, 1854." "A Discourse occasioned by the death of Miss Mercy Tufts, delivered in the Unitarian Church in Quincy, Massachusetts, January 24, 1858." "Liberty versus Romanism, or Romanism hostile to Civil and Religious Liberty—being Two Discourses delivered in the New North Church, Boston," Boston, 1859. Mr. Fuller has also edited a complete series of his sister's life and writings, issued in a standard uniform edition of six volumes, embracing, "Memoirs of Margaret Fuller Ossoli," "Woman in the Nineteenth Century," "At Home and Abroad," "Life Without and Life Within," etc.

In July, 1859, he resigned his pastoral charge of the New North Church in Boston. He now, at the invitation of the Unitarian Church and society of Watertown, Massachusetts, entered upon the pastoral charge in that town.

At the first signs of the great rebellion which broke out after the election of President Lincoln, Mr. Fuller at once took an active part, entering into the cause not only as a patriot, but as a Christian minister, and after the labors of his pulpit, cheerfully hastened to the camps of the recruits, to lend spiritual counsel and cheer to the soldiery. He was unanimously chosen chaplain of the Sixteenth Regiment of Massachusetts Volunteers, as they set forth for the field of conflict. For several months his regiment was stationed at Fortress Monroe. Here he worked hard in the hospital, comforting and praying with the sick and wounded, and, when needed, aiding the surgeons.

Mr. Fuller also kept the public and the friends of his regiment frequently informed of military interests by numerous letters, published in the "Boston Journal," "Traveller," "New York Tribune," "Inquirer," and other papers. These letters were read with much interest, particularly the graphic narrative of the encounter between the "Monitor," and the "Merrimac," of which he was an eye-witness.

After the evacuation of Yorktown, the Sixteenth Massachusetts Regiment was stationed in the front rank of the army advancing upon Richmond, and Mr. Fuller's correspondence contains many exciting sketches of the fierce conflicts, sufferings, and hardships of which that portion of Virginia soil has been the theatre.

At Burnside's attack on Fredericksburg, December 12th, 1862, he volunteered in the hazardous task of crossing the river, and gave his life as the price of his zeal and patriotism.

The vigorous labors of the Rev. Mr. Fuller, as chaplain in the army, have fully illustrated the immense aid which a faithful minister may render in inspiriting soldiers for righteous conflict, encouraging them in the hardships of the campaign, and solacing the sick and wounded. No hardships appalled him, and he always sustained others by his own unflinching courage and his devotion to the great cause he had given himself to serve.

Our Navy.

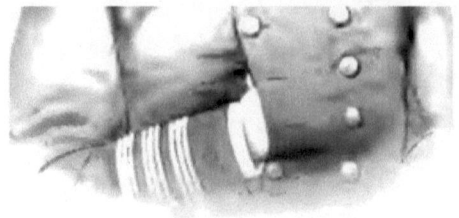

VICE-ADMIRAL D. G. FARRAGUT, U. S. N.

> "Our ship,
> Which, but three glasses since, we gave out split,
> Is tight and yare, and bravely rigged, as when
> We first put out to sea."

DAVID GLASGOW FARRAGUT, is a native of the State of Tennessee, and was appointed to the United States Navy from that State. He entered the service as a midshipman when a mere child, some nine years of age, his warrant bearing date December 17, 1810. He was first on board the Essex, under the redoubtable Commodore David Porter, and served with him also in the expedition around Cape Horn, in 1813. In 1811, this vessel composed one of the coast squadron under Commodore Rodgers, and during the war of 1812 was a terror to the British fleet.

Midshipman Farragut would have been promoted early but from his extreme youth. On one occasion, when it was found necessary to appoint an acting lieutenant to one of Commodore Porter's captures, David Farragut's name was mentioned, but his appointment was opposed on the ground that he was "but a mere boy."

During the year 1821 he passed his examination, and was recommended for promotion. He was then ordered on the West India station. On the 13th of January, 1825, he was commissioned a lieutenant. He was next transferred to the Brandywine. In 1827, he was ordered to the receiving ship at Norfolk, Virginia, which position he held until late in 1828. He was then ordered to the sloop Vandalia, which joined the squadron on the coast of Brazil. On this station he remained about two years, when he again returned to Norfolk. He was retained on the receiving ship at the Norfolk Navy Yard until the year 1833.

He was next ordered to the sloop-of-war Natchez, off the coast of Brazil, on which vessel he held the position of executive officer at the commencement of 1834. From this period until 1851, Commander Farragut was variously employed in duty on the West India station, the Norfolk Navy Yard, the coast of Brazil, and with the Home Squadron. During the year 1851, he was ordered on a service, as Assistant Inspector of Ordnance, being second in command under Commodore Skinner. This position he held until after the end of the year 1853. He was now considered a very efficient ordnance officer.

Another field was at this time opened by the establishment of a new navy-yard at Mare's Island, near San Francisco, California. Commander Farragut was ordered to the chief command of this post. On the 11th of September, 1855, he was commissioned a captain of the United States Navy. He was ordered, in 1858, to the command of the steam sloop, Brooklyn, forming a portion of the Home Squadron, under Flag-officer McCluney.

When the expedition to New Orleans was fitted out, Captain Farragut was appointed by the Navy Department as its Flag Officer. The expedition left Boston on the 20th of February, 1862, with fifteen thousand men on board, commanded by General Butler, and arrived at Ship Island, in Mississippi Sound, on the 23d of March. Again, leaving Ship Island on the 17th of April, Flag Officer Farragut, accompanied by Captain Porter's mortar-fleet, steamed up the Mississippi to operate against New Orleans. The mortar-fleet commenced the bombardment of Fort Jackson, early on the morning of the 18th, and continued it without intermission until the morning of the 24th, when the squadron got into line to pass the Forts, at half-past 3, A. M. In an hour and ten minutes after the vessels had weighed anchor, they had passed the forts, under a most terrific fire, which they returned with interest. During the passage, the mortar fleet rained down shells on Fort Jackson, to try to keep the men from the guns, keeping them comparatively quiet. The Winona was compelled to retire, and the Itasca was fairly riddled, and was shot through her boiler. Captain Bailey, commanding the Division of the Red, led in the Cayuga, and was attacked by three large rebel steamers, one of which he sunk. The Mississippi was attacked by the famous "Hollins' Ram," which she destroyed after a terrible conflict. During the fight, a fire-raft came into collision with the Flag-ship, Hartford, but no material damage was done to her. But by far, the Nelson of this terrific conflict was Captain Charles S. Boggs, of the Varuna, which was also in the Division of the Red. On passing the forts, he found his vessel the leading one, and surrounded by the rebel steamers. Steering as close to them as possible, he gave to each a broadside as he passed, "driving one on shore and leaving four others in flames." Leaking badly, he was soon after attacked by an iron-clad, but repulsed him by planting a couple of broadsides into him, that set him on fire. The Varuna was now on fire, also, and while putting out the flames, the steamer was crushed by another iron-clad, which, in giving him another blow, received a full complement of shot and shell that drove her ashore in flames. But the Varuna was sinking, and just as the decks went under, Captain Boggs gave a broadside to his first opponent, who sank at the same instant.

Having destroyed eleven Rebel steamers, Flag Officer Farragut passed up the river, and, after destroying four forts above the city, took possession of New Orleans on the 29th of April,—the day after the surrender of Forts Jackson and St. Philip to Captain Porter,—and landed General Butler, who took command of the Department of the Gulf, with the city as his headquarters.

On the 30th of July, 1862, he was appointed a Rear Admiral, ranking first on the active list.

REAR-ADMIRAL S. H. STRINGHAM, U.S.N.

> "The flower of our brave for the combat combined,
> Their watchword, humanity's vow;—
> Not a sea-boy that fought in that cause, but mankind
> Owes a garland to honor his brow!"

SILAS HORTON STRINGHAM was born in Middletown, Orange county, New York, on the 7th of November, 1798. He entered the navy as a midshipman in his thirteenth year, and was ordered to the "President," Commodore John Rogers.

There were already signs of the coming storm; and for the next four years the young midshipman found naval life no holiday sport. On the 16th of May, 1811, occurred that memorable fight between the "President" and the English corvette "Little Belt," which was one of the immediate causes of the War of 1812. The "President" had also a fight, in June, 1812, with the "Belvidere," a British frigate.

In 1814 young Stringham was assigned to the "Guerriere," on which he served for a year, when he was ordered to the "Spark," one of the vessels of Commodore Decatur's Algerine squadron. In 1817, Lieutenant Stringham was transferred to the "Erie," and in the fall of 1818 to the "Peacock," which soon afterwards returned to the United States. In 1819 he was ordered to the "Cyane," and convoyed the ship "Elizabeth," which carried to the African coast the first settlers to the future Republic of Liberia. On their arrival, each lieutenant was put in command of a boat to board vessels supposed to be slavers. Stringham captured two, the "Endymion" of Baltimore, and the "Esperanza," a Spanish vessel. Taking one of these vessels, he captured two others, the "Plattsburg" and the "Science." He was then made prize-commodore, and brought his prizes to New York, where they were condemned.

In 1821 he was ordered to the "Hornet" as first-lieutenant, and on the West India station captured a notorious pirate-ship and a slaver. In 1822 he was ordered to the "Cyane," under Commodore Creighton, and formed a part of the Mediterranean squadron. From 1825 to 1829 he spent at the Brooklyn Navy Yard, actively engaged in fitting out war vessels. In 1829 he was assigned to the "Peacock," and sent in search of the missing sloop-of-war "Hornet." He was then appointed to the command of the "Falmouth," and ordered to Carthagena. Returning to New York in 1830, the next five years were spent in shore service; and in 1835 he was ordered to the command of the "John Adams," then in the Mediterranean squadron. In 1837 he again returned to New York, and was appointed second in command at the Brooklyn Navy Yard. In 1842 he was ordered to the razee "Independence," and in 1843 appointed commander of the Brooklyn Navy Yard, where he remained till 1846.

REAR-ADMIRAL S. H. STRINGHAM, U. S. N.

At the commencement of the Mexican War he was ordered to the "Ohio," and sailed from Boston to Vera Cruz. He took an active part in the bombardment of the fortress of San Juan de Ulloa. After the reduction of the fort, the "Ohio" returned to New York, and on her way called at Havana, being the first American ship-of-the-line which had ever entered that port. On his return to New York, Captain Stringham proceeded at once to Rio Janeiro, where he was put in command of the squadron. In 1851 he was made commander of the Norfolk Navy Yard, and in April, 1852, assigned to the command of the Mediterranean squadron. In July, 1855, he returned to the United States, and was assigned to the command of the Charleston Navy Yard, which he held till May, 1859.

In March, 1861, he was ordered to Washington as a member of a naval court-martial, and on special duty, and while there was appointed flag-officer of the Atlantic blockading squadron, and ordered to the "Minnesota" as his flag-ship.

In the summer of 1861, Commodore Stringham was honored with the preparation of the first of those combined naval and military expeditions which have crowned the American navy with such glory. On the 26th of August the fleet, consisting of the "Minnesota," "Wabash," "Monticello," "Pawnee," and "Harriet Lane," sailed from Hampton Roads for Hatteras Inlet. The "Susquehanna" and the "Cumberland" were ordered also to join the expedition, which they did the next day. There were also a number of chartered steamers, transports, etc., which carried the troops intended to take part in the expedition.

On the morning of the 28th of August an attack was made upon the forts, and the bombardment of Fort Clark was continued till half-past one P. M., when both forts hauled down their flags, and the garrison of Fort Clark escaped to Fort Hatteras. The fleet ceased firing, and the "Monticello" was sent into the inlet to discover whether the forts intended to surrender. When within six hundred yards of Fort Hatteras, the occupants of that fort commenced firing upon her. Perceiving this, Flag-Officer Stringham came to her assistance with the "Wabash," "Susquehanna," and "Minnesota," and soon compelled them to cease firing. The next morning the fleet renewed its fire upon Fort Hatteras, dropping almost every shell from their heavy guns inside the fort. At ten minutes past eleven a white flag was displayed from the fort, and the preliminaries having been agreed upon, the garrison, consisting of seven hundred and fifteen men, surrendered to Flag-Officer Stringham and General Butler, who commanded the land forces. Not a man belonging to the fleet was killed. For this brilliant affair, Flag-Officer Stringham received the thanks of the Government. On the 23d of September, 1861, he was, at his own request, relieved from his command.

On the 17th of July, 1862, he was made a rear-admiral on the retired list, and in August and September was president of the naval commission to locate a new navy yard.

REAR-ADMIRAL L. M. GOLDSBOROUGH, U.S.N.

> "'My letters say, a hundred and seven galleys.'
> 'And mine, a hundred and forty.'
> 'And mine, two hundred :
> But though they jump not on a just account
> (As in these cases, where the aim reports,
> 'Tis oft with difference), yet do they all confirm
> A Turkish fleet, and bearing up to Cyprus.'"

Louis Malecherbes Goldsborough was born in the city of Washington, February 18th, 1805. At the breaking out of the war with Great Britain, in 1812, he then being but seven years of age, waited upon the Honorable Paul Hamilton, then Secretary of the Navy, and solicited from him an appointment as a midshipman. Without even the aid or knowledge of his father, he received it, his warrant bearing date June 18th, 1812. His father was a man of such a nice sense of honor that he would not allow his son to draw pay while he was yet too young to perform duty, and accordingly waited upon the secretary, and while thanking him for the appointment, told him his son could not receive any pay until he entered active service. He wore his uniform and went to school in Washington for several years, finally going to sea in 1817.

His first cruise was in the "Franklin," seventy-four, the flag-ship of Commodore Stewart, then in command of the Mediterranean squadron. She sailed from Philadelphia, October 14th, 1817, having on board the Honorable Richard Rush, minister to England.

His services as a midshipman were varied, in ship and squadron. On the 13th of January, 1825, he was promoted to a lieutenancy. When in this capacity, on board of the brig "Porpoise," and on the 16th of October, 1827, he distinguished himself by his dashing and gallant capture of a piratical brig, by boarding her, and driving the pirates into their boats, and finally to the shore, keeping a running fire upon, and producing great slaughter among them. In September, 1840, while in command of the "Enterprise," he captured at Bahia, Brazil, the pirate "Malik-Adhel, with a valuable cargo, which he sent into Baltimore.

When about twenty-one years of age, having an unofficial opportunity of visiting Europe, he made an extended pedestrian tour in France and Switzerland, spending a fortnight with the Marquis de Lafayette.

REAR-ADMIRAL L. M. GOLDSBOROUGH, U. S. N.

He has commanded, at various times, the following vessels: "Ohio," seventy-four; "Cumberland," forty-four; "Congress," forty-four; "Marian," sixteen; "Enterprise," ten. On the 8th of September, 1841, he received his commission as a commander in the United States navy.

From 1853 to 1857 he was superintendent of the Naval Academy at Annapolis — a position for which his studies and his mathematical and executive ability at that time fitted him in an eminent degree. During his administration many important improvements and changes were made, and the general efficiency of the institution was greatly increased, and he received the special commendation of the Secretary of the Navy.

After being relieved from this duty he was ordered to form a portion of a board to revise the "Ordnance Manual" for the use of naval officers.

In 1858 he was ordered to the command of the frigate "Congress," forty-four, the flag-ship of Commodore Sands, on the Brazil station. He returned in that ship just after the opening of hostilities in 1861; and after being unemployed for a short time, he was, through the influence of Secretary Chase, appointed to the command of the North Atlantic blockading squadron, hoisting his broad pennant on board of the "Minnesota." He participated in the combined attack on Roanoke Island, and figured extensively in that affair. During his absence the "Merrimac" made her celebrated raid into Hampton Roads.

He was commissioned as a captain September 14th, 1855, and was appointed a rear-admiral by act of July 17th, 1862. In the summer of 1862, Admiral Goldsborough was relieved of his command by Acting Rear-Admiral Samuel Phillip Lee, a relative of Postmaster-General Blair, and he went into retirement, but is engaged in compiling the circulars issued by the Navy Department.

His total sea service in 1861 was seventeen years and ten months; shore duty, eleven years and nine months; unemployed, eighteen years and eleven months. Total time in the service, forty-eight years and six months.

REAR-ADMIRAL S. F. DU PONT, U.S.N.

> "Three times that triple dance he fearless led;
> Three times that circuit, that ellipse so dread;
> Three times, 'mid splintering spar and falling dead,
> He led the merciless path;
> Three times his frigates and his gunboats well
> Replied, with hot shot and with bursting shell,
> Enfilading those walls, that quaked and fell
> Beneath the scorching wrath!"

SAMUEL F. DU PONT entered the naval service of the United States on the 19th of December, 1815. Although he was born in the State of New Jersey, he received his appointment into the navy from the State of Delaware.

In 1817 he was attached to the "Franklin," seventy-four, and remained in her the cruise. In 1821 he was located at the Philadelphia navy yard, and in the following year he was ordered to the frigate "Constitution." In 1823 he was a midshipman on board the frigate "Congress."

In 1825, standing at the head of his letter in the class of midshipmen, he was attached to the "North Carolina," seventy-four, of the Mediterranean squadron, where he remained the entire cruise.

On the 28th of April, 1826, he was promoted to be a lieutenant. In 1828 he was granted a leave of absence, which was ended by his being ordered to the sloop-of-war "Ontario," eighteen, attached to the Mediterranean squadron, where he remained until 1833, and on his return home, he was granted a leave of absence.

In June, 1836, he commanded the sloop-of-war "Warren," eighteen, then attached to the West India squadron, under Commodore A. J. Dallas; retaining the command but one year, he returned home and was granted a leave of absence.

In 1839 he was ordered to the "Ohio," seventy-four, attached to the Mediterranean squadron. He remained in this ship a three years' cruise, returning to the United States in 1842.

On the 28th of October, 1842, he received his commission as a commander, and in December, 1843, he was ordered to the command of the brig "Perry," ten, attached to the East India squadron. He returned home in 1844, and in October, 1845, he was ordered to the command of the frigate "Congress," forty-four, at that time the flagship of Commodore R. F. Stockton. She carried out Mr. Ten Eyck, United States Commissioner to the Sandwich Islands, and also Mr. Surell, United States Consul to the same islands.

REAR-ADMIRAL S. F. DU PONT, U.S.N.

In July, 1846, he commanded the sloop-of-war "Cyane," and was attached to the Pacific squadrons, under Commodores W. B. Shubrick and Thomas A. C. Jones; he returned in October, 1848, and was granted a leave of absence. In 1851 he was ordered to the command of the receiving-ship at Philadelphia. In 1853 he was detached and appointed a member of the Lighthouse Board, which position he occupied until the latter part of 1855.

On the 14th of September, 1855, he was promoted to a captaincy, and in June, 1856, he was ordered to the command of the flag-ship "Minnesota."

In 1860 he was in command of the Philadelphia navy yard, a post which he filled with great honor to himself and credit to his country.

At the formation of the celebrated South Atlantic blockading squadron, he was placed over it as the flag-officer, and most nobly did he do the duty assigned to him in the capture of the rebel forts at Port Royal, South Carolina. Leaving Fortress Monroe on the 29th of October, 1861, with fifty vessels, including the transports with General Sherman's army, he arrived off Hilton Head on the 3d of November. At nine o'clock on the morning of the 7th, the fleet got under way, and soon after the rebels opened fire. The plan of the attack was simple and effective, being for the ships to steam in an ellipse, running close to Fort Walker on one shore as they came down the river, and near Fort Beauregard on the other as they went up. The flag-ship "Wabash" leading, swept down in line, and "delivered their compliments at Hilton Head, in the shape of ten-second shells, while the lively gunboats put in the punctuation points for the benefit of the rebel commodore," at the same time enfilading the two batteries. The firing now became incessant, and a perfect shower of shot and shell fell inside the rebel forts for over four hours, during which the national fleet delivered over two thousand rounds. At about three o'clock, P. M., the rebels fled in the greatest confusion, leaving everything behind them. Not one of the national vessels was disabled or destroyed, though several of them were badly cut up.

His squadron has always been noted for its efficiency, and all the qualifications necessary to render it of the highest order.

On the 16th of July, 1862, Congress passed the "Act to Establish and Equalize the Grades of Line Officers of the United States Navy," and on the following day, Captains Farragut, Goldsborough, Dupont and Foote were appointed rear-admirals on the active list.

Admiral Du Pont's service is as follows: Sea service, over twenty-three years; shore duty, eight years and six months; unemployed, nearly fifteen years—giving a total of nearly forty-seven years in the service of his country.

He is one who, though past what is usually termed the prime of life, is yet possessed of all the vigor and bodily strength which usually characterize younger men.

REAR-ADMIRAL ANDREW H. FOOTE, U.S.N.

> "The glory of his life was set
>   Unto a measure high and grand;
> The lofty anthem lingers yet
>   In haunting echoes through the land;
> And, greeted with a triumph tone,
>   He stood, a conqueror—alone!"

ANDREW H. FOOTE, the honored son of the Honorable Samuel A. Foote, is a native of New Haven, Connecticut, where his family now reside. He early exhibited a strong inclination to join the Navy, and in 1822 he entered as midshipman. In 1830 he received a lieutenant's commission. In the following years he cruised in the Mediterranean, under Commodore Patterson, in the seventy-four-gun ship Delaware. In 1839, under Commodore Read, he made the voyage around the world. During the Mexican War he was stationed at the Charleston Navy Yard, engaged in fitting out vessels to coöperate with our army. In the latter part of 1849 he was appointed to the command of the brig Perry, and ordered to join the American squadron off the coast of Africa. There he proved one of the most efficient officers in the service in suppressing the slave-trade. Captain Foote formed one of the famous "Retiring Board," appointed by President Pierce to inquire into the efficiency of the officers of the Navy.

His last cruise was from 1856 to 1858, off the coast of China and Japan. The firing upon a boat's crew of his men by the Chinese brought out that spirit of intrepid daring which has distinguished him in the present campaign. Without waiting orders he assumed the responsibility of avenging the injury. With his twenty-two guns and three hundred men he attacked and breached the celebrated Barrier forts, regular fortifications of solid granite, and garrisoned by five thousand men.

At the outbreak of the great rebellion he was stationed at the Brooklyn Navy Yard. He superintended the outfit of the blockading squadron until he was transferred to the Western waters. There, receiving great assistance from the energetic Fremont while in command, the building of the gunboat fleet progressed rapidly; and at length, on the night of the 5th of February, 1862, the gallant flag officer steamed away from Cairo, so silently that the nation hardly knew that he was gone until his cannon were heard at the walls of Fort Henry. This fort was held by the rebel General Tilghman, with about six thousand men. Commodore Foote, with seven gunboats, arrived near the fort on the 6th, and opened the bombardment about noon. After a vigorous cannonade of an hour and a quarter, the fort surrendered, and the land forces took possession. Flag Officer Foote then returned to Cairo, and prepared for an assault on Fort Donelson.

In his report of February 15th he says: "I made an attack on Fort Donelson yesterday, at three o'clock P. M., with four iron-clad gunboats and two wooden ones, and after one hour and a quarter severe fighting (the latter part of the day within less than four hundred yards of the fort), the wheel of this vessel and the tiller of the Louisville were shot away, rendering the two boats unmanageable. There were fifty-four killed and wounded in this attack, which we have reason to suppose would, in fifteen minutes more, could the action have been continued, have resulted in the capture of the fort bearing upon us, as the enemy was running from his batteries when the two gunboats helplessly drifted down the river from disabled steering apparatus, as the relieving tackles could not steer the vessels in the strong current."

After the evacuation of Columbus, the Confederate forces which had occupied that position fell down the Mississippi to Island No. 10, about forty-five miles below Columbus. On the 16th of March, Captain Foote began the investment with the Federal gunboats. On the 20th he sent a dispatch, saying, "Island No. 10 is harder to conquer than Columbus, as the island shores are lined with forts, each one commanding the one above it. I am gradually approaching the island, but still do not hope for much until the occurrence of certain events which promise success." These "events" comprehended the cutting off, at New Madrid, of all access by the river from below; the digging of a canal through a swamp on the main-land, west of the island, through which a part of our gunboats could pass below the island, and the passage of the river from the Missouri to the Kentucky shore in the face of the enemy's batteries. These operations were successfully carried out, a brisk bombardment being all the while kept up, and everything was in readiness for an assault, when, at midnight of the 7th of April, two rebel officers boarded our boats with orders to surrender the island to the commander of the naval expedition.

Indefatigable still, he left New Madrid on the 12th, to attack Fort Pillow and Memphis. Day after day the bombardment was kept up. But the brave old Commodore was gradually sinking under the debilitating effects of his wound received at Fort Donelson, and, though loth to leave his brave companions, he was obliged, on the 9th of May, to relinquish the command to Captain Davis, and return to his home.

On the 16th of July, the President signed the "Act to Establish and Equalize the grades of Line Officers of the United States Navy;" and on the 30th, appointed Captain Foote a Rear-Admiral,—ranking the fourth on the active list. A few days after, the Bureau of Construction was established, and Admiral Foote, having in a measure recovered his impaired health, was put at its head.

Admiral Foote commands confidence and esteem, not only for his efficient soldierly ability, but for the rarer virtues of the Christian. Combining military ardor with religious enthusiasm, he has been termed the Christian warrior—the Cromwell of America.

REAR-ADMIRAL C. H. DAVIS, U. S. N.

> "Ye sons of Columbia, who bravely have fought
> For those rights which unstain'd from your sires had descended,
> May you long taste the blessings your valor has bought,
> And your sons reap the soil which their fathers defended."

CHARLES HENRY DAVIS is a native of the State of Massachusetts, from which State he entered the navy on the 12th of August, 1823.

His first sea service was performed in the frigate "United States," attached to the Pacific squadron. In 1826 he was attached to the sloop-of-war "Boston," and in 1828 to the sloop-of-war "Erie," on the West India station. He passed his examination and joined the sloop-of-war "Ontario," on the same station, in 1830. On the 3d of March, 1831, he was promoted to a lieutenancy, still remaining on board of the "Ontario." In 1832 he returned home and was granted a leave of absence.

In 1834 he was ordered to the sloop-of-war "Vincennes," of the Brazil squadron, and after serving on her for two years, he was granted a leave of absence in 1836; the following year we find him recruiting for the Brazil squadron, and then ordered to the razee "Independence," where he remained until 1840, when he returned home. In 1842 he was ordered to the rendezvous in Boston; during the following year he was assigned to duty on the Coast Survey, remaining there several years. In 1847 he commanded the "Gallatin," United States Coast Surveying schooner, and two years later, the "Bibb," United States Coast Surveying steamer. In 1851, an appropriation was made by the Federal Government for the improvement of Charleston harbor, and at the request of South Carolina, a commission of navy and army officers was appointed to superintend the work. Captain Davis was one of the commission, and for three or four years was engaged in these operations. From that time to 1857, he was on special duty at the Cambridge Observatory. On the 12th of June, 1854, he received the commission of a commander in the United States navy.

In 1857 he was ordered to the command of the sloop-of-war "St. Marys," twenty-two, of the Pacific squadron, under Commodore Long. In 1859 he was ordered home, and was appointed superintendent of the "Nautical Almanac," which post he filled until the breaking out of the Southern rebellion. By reason of the desertion of a large number of naval officers, he was made a captain in 1861, and ordered to the flag-ship "Wabash," as the fleet captain under Flag-Officer DuPont. In this position he distinguished himself on every occasion.

At the battle of Port Royal, he was noted for his great courage and discretion, which brought forth the admiration and commendation of all. Flag-Officer Du Pont says in his official report to the Secretary of the Navy: "The Department is aware that all the aids to navigation had been removed, and the bar lies ten miles seaward, with no features on the shore line with sufficient prominence to make any bearing reliable. But owing to the skill of Commander Davis, the fleet captain, and Mr. Boutelle, the able assistant of the Coast Survey, in charge of the steamer 'Vixen,' the channel was immediately found, sounded out and buoyed." Captain Davis subsequently led several minor but successful expeditions along the coast.

On the 20th of November, 1861, the "Stone fleet" sailed from Boston for Charleston harbor, where it arrived about the middle of December, under command of Captain Davis. This fleet was composed of old hulks of whaling vessels, freighted with granite. Its object was the effectual obstruction of the harbor of Charleston. This very difficult and delicate operation Captain Davis successfully accomplished on the 19th and 20th of December.

His services being duly appreciated, he was ordered to the command of the naval flotilla on the Mississippi River, to take the place of the gallant Foote, who from the nature of wounds received in battle, was unable to retain his command.

The operations before Vicksburg were carried on with the flotilla under the command of Commodore Davis. His energy and tact were always noted; but owing to various insurmountable difficulties, he was not able to reduce the place, although assisted by Admiral Farragut.

When Acting Rear-Admiral Porter returned from the lower Mississippi, Commodore Davis was detached from his command, and ordered to Washington as the Chief of Bureau of Navigation. He now ranks among the acting rear-admirals.

He has seen about twenty years' sea service, sixteen years on shore and other duty, and about five years unemployed.

Massachusetts may well be proud of her Davis, while our country will ever hold him in high esteem.

He is probably one of the most scientific men of the United States navy, or of the age.

He is quick and agile in his motions, a brave officer, a fine gentleman, and a pleasant, social companion.

REAR-ADMIRAL D. D. PORTER, U. S. N.

"Natura lo fece, è poi ruppa la stampa."

David D. Porter, the commander of the Mississippi flotilla, is the son of the famous Commodore David Porter of the "Essex," and was born about the year 1814. In 1829 he entered the navy as midshipman on board the "Constellation," and served six years on that ship and the "United States." In 1835 he passed his examination, and served six years as past midshipman on the Coast Survey. In 1841 he was commissioned a lieutenant, and served with that rank on board the "Congress" for four years. After a brief period of service at the Observatory at Washington, he was placed on active duty under Commodore Tatnall in the Gulf of Mexico, and took a leading part in the naval operations of the Mexican War. In 1849 he was allowed to take command of one of the Pacific Mail Company's steamers, and remained several years in the service of that company.

At the beginning of the year 1861 he was under orders to join the Coast Survey on the Pacific, but, fortunately, had not left when the rebellion broke out. His name at this time stood number six on the list of lieutenants. The resignation of several naval traitors left room for his advancement, and the Naval Register for August 31, 1861, places him number seventy-seven on the list of commanders. He was placed in command of the steam sloop-of-war "Powhatan," a vessel of about twenty-five hundred tons, and armed with eleven guns. After doing blockading duty for some time, he left that ship to take special charge of the mortar expedition.

The active part he took in the reduction of the forts below New Orleans will make his name ever memorable in connection with the mortar fleet, or "bummers," as the sailors term them.

In his report of April 25th, 1862, he says: "We commenced the bombardment of Fort Jackson on the 18th, and continued it without intermission until the squadron made preparations to move. . . . . In an hour and ten minutes after the vessels had weighed anchor they had passed the forts, under a most terrific fire, which they returned with interest. The mortar fleet rained down shells on Fort Jackson, to try and keep the men from the guns, while the steamers of the mortar fleet poured in shrapnell upon the water battery commanding the approach at a short distance, keeping them comparatively quiet. When the last vessel of ours could be seen, among the fire and smoke, to pass the battery, signal was made to the mortars to cease firing, and the flotilla steamers were directed to retire from a contest that would soon become unequal . . . . The mortar fleet have been very much exposed and under a heavy fire for six days, during which time they kept the shells going without intermission. One of them, the "Maria I. Carlton," was sunk by a shot passing down through her magazine and then through her bottom. The flotilla lost but one man killed and six wounded. The bearing of the officers and men was worthy of the highest praise. They never once flagged, during a period of six days, never had an accident to one of the vessels by firing, and when shell and shot were flying thick above them, showed not the least desire to have the vessels moved to a place of safety."

Again, in his report of the 30th, he says: "Fort Jackson is a perfect wreck. Everything in the shape of a building in and about it was burned up by the mortar shells, and over 1,800 shells fell in the work proper, to say nothing of those which burst over and around it. I devoted but little attention to Fort St. Philip, knowing that when Jackson fell, St. Philip would follow."

After the capture of New Orleans he, with his fleet, went up the Mississippi River, and was engaged in several affairs on that river, including that of Vicksburg. From that place he was ordered to the James River, and returned in the "Octorara." When off Charleston, on his way to Fortress Monroe, he fell in with and captured the Anglo-rebel steamer "Tubal Cain." He has now been appointed to the supreme control of all the naval forces on the Mississippi River, with the rank of acting rear-admiral. The forces under his orders, in vessels, guns, and men, will be larger than ever before under the command of any United States naval officer. His squadron will be distinct in every way from that of Admiral Farragut, who will still command the Western Gulf blockading squadron.

Commander Porter is a man of wiry, muscular frame, handsome features, of medium height, and, a few years ago, universally admitted to be the strongest man in the navy. He is about forty-five years old, and exhibits but few marks of age. He is married to a sister of Captain C. P. Patterson, formerly of San Francisco, by whom he has several children. He is most truly "a worthy son of a worthy sire."

COMMODORE CHARLES WILKES, U.S.N.

> "You know them envys thet the Rebbles sent,
> An' Cap'n Wilkes he borried o' the Trent!"

CHARLES WILKES entered the naval service of his country on the 1st of January, 1818. He is a native of the State of New York, and was appointed from his native State. In 1819–'20 he was attached to the frigate "Guerriere," forty-four. In 1822 he joined the "Franklin," seventy-four, and remained in her an entire cruise. In 1824–'25 he was on a furlough. In the latter year he was passed for promotion, and was granted a leave of absence. On the 28th of April, 1826, he was promoted to a lieutenant. In 1829 he was attached to the schooner "Porpoise," in the Mediterranean; on his return, he waited orders until 1831, when he was ordered to the sloop-of-war "Boston," also attached to the Mediterranean squadron.

In 1833 he was attached to the surveying expedition at work on the waters of the Narraganset Bay, and the following year he was at Washington at the Observatory, in charge of the chronometers of the navy.

In 1836 he was on special duty, and in the following year he commanded the brig "Porpoise," then on surveying duty. His acknowledged skill as a navigator, and his admitted scientific attainments, caused him to be selected by the Government in 1838, to command the celebrated "Wilkes' Exploring Expedition." His command consisted of two sloops-of-war, a brig, and two tenders; he was raised to the grade of captain.

Leaving the United States, he doubled Cape Horn, crossed over to Polynesia, Van Diemen's Land and Australia, advancing as high as the sixty-first degree of south latitude. He then visited the Feejee Islands and Borneo, and returned to New York in 1842, touching en route at Singapore and the Cape of Good Hope.

The discovery of a southern continent, along the shores of which he sailed for several days, added much to previous geographical knowledge, which was exceedingly limited, of high southern latitudes—latitudes which were subsequently visited by Sir James Ross, of the British navy, and with cool impudence, he sought to appropriate to his own country by re-naming the extensive coasts baptized by Wilkes. The expedition was absent four years, and on its return, Wilkes published the results of his observations in a very ably written work, comprising five octavo volumes, entitled "A Narrative of the United States Exploring Expedition."

For his labors he was rewarded by the Geographical Society of London, in 1848, with a gold medal, as a token of their appreciation of his labors in the cause of science. More recently, Captain Wilkes published a valuable work, entitled "Western America," which is replete with statistical details and valuable geographical facts, and maps relating to California and Oregon.

As Captain Wilkes was returning from the coast of Africa in the fall of 1861, in command of the "San Jacinto," he learned at Cienfuegos that the "Theodora" had run the blockade at Charleston, and arrived at the Havana with the rebel commissioners, Mason and Slidell, and their secretaries, Eustis and McFarland, all of whom were to take passage to England in the British mail steamer "Trent." Captain Wilkes at once determined to capture them, and therefore lay in wait for the steamer in the Old Bahama Channel. About noon on the 8th of November, 1861, the "Trent" hove in sight. Stopping her by firing a shot across her bows, Captain Wilkes sent Lieutenant D. M. Fairfax to board her with two armed boats. After some slight difficulty, the rebel commissioners and their secretaries were put into the boat, and brought on board the "San Jacinto" by Lieutenant Fairfax. Captain Wilkes arrived in New York harbor on the 18th, and immediately went from thence to Boston harbor, where his prisoners were confined in Fort Warren. England claimed this as a violation of the neutrality laws, and demanded the release of the rebel envoys. Sooner than fight Great Britain in this period of our country's peril, England's claim was complied with, and the captives of Fort Warren delivered to the British authorities on the 1st of January, 1862.

After the "Trent" affair, Commodore Wilkes remained quiet until the army of the Potomac had nearly reached Richmond by the way of the James River, when he was ordered to the command of the James River flotilla. He remained here but a short time, when he was placed in command of a special squadron to prevent Anglo-rebel vessels from running into the Southern ports, and to pursue and destroy any rebel privateers that should cruise among the West India Islands. On the 16th of July, 1862, Congress passed the bill "To Equalize the Grades of Line Officers of the United States Navy." On the following day the President appointed, and the Senate confirmed the appointment, of Captain Wilkes to the rank of commodore. Commodore Wilkes has been in the naval service about forty-five years, eleven of which have been in sea service, twenty-six on shore duty, and nearly seven years unemployed.

By virtue of his command, he received an appointment as acting rear-admiral, when he took command of the flying squadron.

COMMANDER JOHN L. WORDEN, U.S.N.

> "God! with a handful of such hearted men
> To beard the wolf of treason in his den;
> Men quick to plan, and strong to act—and then
> Europe shall ring our triumphs back again!"

JOHN LORIMER WORDEN was born at Mount Pleasant, Westchester county, New York, on the 12th of March, 1818. In 1827 he removed with his parents to Fishkill, Dutchess county, New York.

He received his appointment as midshipman from that county on the 10th of January, 1834. Midshipman Worden made his maiden cruise in the sloop-of-war "Erie" to the coast of Brazil, and remained in her from 1834 to 1837. On his return he was ordered to the sloop-of-war "Cyane." She sailed from Boston June 24th, 1838, under the command of Commander John Percival, for the Mediterranean squadron, under Commodore Isaac Hull. He returned, and was examined for promotion in 1840, and then was ordered to the store-ship "Relief," Lieutenant J. S. Nichols, sailing from New York, December 1st, 1840, with stores for the Pacific squadron. Arriving on the station, he was transferred to the sloop-of-war "Dale," Commander T. A. Dornin, returning in her to Philadelphia, where they arrived October 20th, 1843.

He then was ordered to the National Observatory at Washington, District of Columbia, where he remained until the breaking out of the Mexican War, when he was ordered to the store-ship "Southampton," the supply vessel of the Pacific squadron. In November, 1846, he had been promoted to a lieutenancy, and while on the Pacific station was transferred to the following ships: razee "Independence," sloop "Warren," and liner "Ohio," returning in the latter vessel to Boston, April 27th, 1850. He then was ordered again to duty at the observatory, where he remained about two years.

He was then ordered to the "Cumberland" frigate, the flag-ship of Commodore S. H. Stringham, sailing from Boston, May 17th, 1852, for the Mediterranean station. He was transferred to and came home in the sloop-of-war "Levant," arriving in the United States in 1855. In the latter part of 1855 he was ordered, as the first-lieutenant, to the Brooklyn Navy Yard, where he remained until August, 1858. From that time until November, 1860, he was the first-lieutenant of the frigate "Savannah," attached to the home squadron, and cruising in the Gulf of Mexico.

On the 6th of April, 1861, he was ordered to report at Washington for duty in the

COMMANDER JOHN L. WORDEN, U. S. N.

bureau of detail; but he asked to be relieved from it, and was ordered to proceed with dispatches to Captain Adams, of the frigate "Sabine," then lying off Pensacola.

Lieutenant Worden left Washington on the morning of the 7th of April on his hazardous mission, via Richmond, Montgomery. Finding that there was a speedy prospect of hostilities commencing, he determined, while on his way from Atlanta to Montgomery, to commit the dispatches to memory, and then destroy the written documents. Having done so, he was prepared to give Captain Adams his instructions without fear that the rebels could learn of their import.

He arrived at Pensacola on the morning of April 11th, and was ordered under a temporary arrest; but General Bragg, who commanded the Confederate forces, gave him a pass which enabled him to go on board of the "Sabine." Providentially for the fate of Fort Pickens, a gale prevented its capture by Bragg, and it detained Lieutenant Worden until the 12th before he could get on board of the gunboat "Wyandotte," which was to convey him to the frigate. After delivering his dispatches he returned to Pensacola, and took the train for Montgomery unmolested; but the following day, and when within five miles of Montgomery, he was arrested by a telegraphic order from Bragg, and was placed in the charge of the marshal until the 15th, when he was thrown into the county jail, where, treated as a prisoner of war, he remained until the 14th of November, when he was released on a parole, and ordered to report to the adjutant-general at Richmond. From here he was sent to Norfolk, and exchanged for Lieutenant Sharp of the Confederate States navy, captured at Fort Hatteras.

After reporting at Washington, being in feeble health, he was ordered to the rendezvous at New York, where he remained until February, 1862. He was then ordered to the Ericsson iron-clad battery "Monitor," a new and novel piece of naval architecture. After a perilous voyage, she arrived in Hampton Roads on the evening of the 8th of March, and just after the raid of the rebel iron-clad "Merrimac." On the morning of the 9th this untried vessel set out to meet the terror of the loyal fleet, and, without any hesitancy on the part of Worden, she engaged her formidable antagonist. The action commenced warily on the part of both vessels, until each, becoming emboldened by their prowess, drew in the line of battle and engaged each other as closely as possible. The engagement was witnessed by thousands, and was the first fight of iron-clads in the history of navies. It will be conceded by any sensible person that it required no ordinary courage to enter such an action in an untried vessel. The result is too well known for us to enter into its details in this place. During the engagement, a shell from the "Merrimac" struck and burst on the pilot-house of the "Monitor," and the unexploded grains of powder filled the eyes of Lieutenant Worden, and he was carried below insensible and blind. For over a month he was blind; but subsequently he regained his sight, and now sees as well as ever, excepting a slight mist which at times troubles him. After his recovery he was ordered on special duty in connection with the new iron-clads, and then ordered to the command of the "Montauk."

S. B. BRITTAN, Jr., U.S.N.

"Dulce et decorum est, pro Patria mori."

SAMUEL BYRON BRITTAN, JR., was born in Bridgeport, Connecticut, on the 17th of June, 1845. He was a brave, sincere, and high-minded youth, of prepossessing person and manners, and was alike admired and beloved. His symmetrical and muscular proportions, and his manly deportment, not less than his courage and intelligence, presented all the characteristics of an early and vigorous manhood.

On the fall of Sumter, young Brittan, though less than sixteen years of age, manifested an intense desire to enlist as a private soldier in the Union army, insisting that he could better go than those who had family responsibilities; but his father was unwilling, owing to his son's extreme youth, and the latter yielded to parental advice. Subsequently, Captain William D. Porter, of the "Essex," offered him the situation of aide and private secretary, and, with the consent of his parents, it was accepted. On the 24th of October, 1861, Flag Officer Foote commissioned him a master's mate in the western gunboat squadron; and on Tuesday, the 12th of November, the young hero bade an affectionate adieu to his parents, his sisters, and his brothers, and left his home at Irvington—alas! never to return.

On the 6th of February, 1862, Flag Officer Foote attacked Fort Henry, and then was fought the death-fight of our brave "boy-hero." Twenty minutes before the surrender of the fort, he was standing forward on the gun-deck, by the side of his brave commander. Captain Porter and his aide were watching the terrific effect of their firing on the rebel fortifications, and engaged in familiar conversation. At this moment, a forty-two-pound shot from the enemy's works, entering directly over the forward port gun, struck the young midshipman, taking off the posterior and coronal portions of his head, and passing on through the bulkhead, designed to protect the machinery, entered the middle boiler, and, releasing the fiery demon within, carried death to several others on board.

The young officer died instantly, while thus nobly employed at the post of duty, and with his face to the foe. One hand was on the shoulder of his commander, to whom he was strongly attached, and with the other he was drawing his cutlass to cheer on the tried men at the guns. His heart was firm, and his spirit fearless, amid the thunder and lightning of the battle-storm; and even at the fatal moment a triumphant smile played over his youthful brow, as if the spirit of victory, that already hovered above the stars and stripes, was mirrored in his countenance. His career was short, and his young life was a pure and willing offering on the altar of his country

BOY BRITTAN.

BY FORCEYTHE WILLSON.

Boy Brittan—only a lad—a fair-haired boy—sixteen,
    In his uniform!
Into the storm—into the roaring jaws of grim
    Fort Henry—
  Boldly bears the Federal flotilla—
    Into the battle-storm!

Boy Brittan is Master's mate aboard of the Essex,
    There he stands buoyant and eager-eyed,
    By the brave Captain's side;
Ready to do and dare—aye, aye, sir, always ready—
    In his country's uniform!
Boom! boom! and now the flag boat sweeps,
    and now the Essex,
    Into the battle-storm!

Boom! Boom! till River, and Fort, and Field,
    are over-clouded
  By the battle's breath; then from the Fort a gleam
And a crashing gun, and the Essex is wrapt and
    shrouded
    In a scalding cloud of steam!

    But victory! victory!
Unto God all praise be ever rendered—
  Unto God all praise and glory be!
  See, boy Brittan, see, Boy, see!
They strike! Hurrah! the Fort has just surrendered!
Shout! shout! my Boy, my warrior Boy!
And wave your cap and clap your hands for joy!
  Cheer answer cheer and bear the cheer about—
Hurrah! hurrah! for the fiery Fort is ours;
  And "Victory!" "Victory!" "Victory!"
    Is the shout.
Shout—for the fiery Fort, and the field, and the
    day, are ours—
  The day is ours—thanks to the brave endeavor
    Of heroes, Boy, like thee;
  The day is ours—the day is ours—
Glory and deathless love to all who shared with thee,
And bravely endured and dared with thee—
  The day is ours—the day is ours—
    Forever!
Glory and love for one and all; but—but—for thee—
  Home! home! a happy "Welcome—welcome
    home" for thee!
    And kisses of love for thee—
And a mother's happy, happy tears, and a virgin's
    bridal wreath of flowers—
    For thee!

    Victory! Victory!
But suddenly wrecked and wrapped in seething steam,
    the Essex

Slowly drifted out of the battle-storm;
Slowly, slowly—down, laden with the dead and
    the dying;
And there, at the Captain's feet, among the dead
    and the dying,
The shot-marred form of a beautiful Boy is lying—
    There in his uniform!

    Laurels and tears for thee, Boy,
    Laurels and tears for thee!
Laurels of light moist with the precious dew
  Of the inmost heart of the Nation's loving heart,
And blest by the balmy breath of the Beautiful
    and the True;
  Moist—moist with the luminous breath of the
    singing spheres
    And the nation's starry tears!
And trembled-touched by the pulse-like gush and start
  Of the universal music of the heart,
    And all deep sympathy.
Laurels and tears for thee, Boy,
  Laurels and tears for thee—
Laurels of light, and tears of love, for evermore,
    For thee.

And laurels of Light and tears of Truth,
    And the Mantle of Immortality;
And the flowers of Love and immortal Youth,
And the tender heart tokens of all true ruth—
    And the everlasting Victory!
  And the breath and bliss of Liberty,
    And the loving kiss of Liberty,
  And the welcoming light of heavenly eyes,
    And the over-calm of God's canopy;
And the infinite love-span of the skies
That cover the Valleys of Paradise—
  For all of the brave who rest with thee;
And for one and all who died with thee,
  And now sleep side by side with thee;
And for every one who lives and dies
  On the solid land or the heaving sea,
    Dear warrior-boy—like thee!

    Oh, the Victory—the Victory
    Belongs to thee!
God ever keeps the brightest crown for such as thou—
    He gives it now to thee!
O Young and Brave, and early and thrice blest:
    Thrice, thrice, thrice blest!
Thy country turns once more to kiss thy youthful brow,
  And takes thee gently, gently, to her breast,
And whispers lovingly: "God bless thee—bless thee now!
    My darling, thou shalt rest!"

www.ingramcontent.com/pod-product-compliance
Lightning Source LLC
Chambersburg PA
CBHW031958300426
44117CB00008B/809